Praise for
Faith Over Fear

"Michael Leach's *Faith Over Fear* provides a compelling story of one man's commitment to the principles of diversity and inclusion from his experience in the NFL to his role in the Biden White House as the first-ever White House Chief Diversity and Inclusion Officer. A powerful story of faith, perseverance, and resilience."

—Anthony Fauci, MD, #1 *New York Times* Bestselling Author and Former Director of the National Institute of Allergy and Infectious Diseases

"*Faith Over Fear* is a powerful story and guiding light for anyone seeking courage, clarity, and purpose. With heart and wisdom, Michael Leach shares a message that transcends backgrounds and borders, reminding us that even in uncertain times, we all have the power to persevere. Every reader—no matter where they're from—will find a piece of themselves in these pages and walk away inspired to rise."

—Michelle Kwan, Two-Time Olympic Medalist and Former US Ambassador

"*Faith Over Fear* is a call to conscience. Michael Leach doesn't just tell his story—he invites us into the sacred tension between who we've been and who we're becoming. In a world that rewards division and ego, this book urges us to choose unity, purpose, and alignment. It is both a bridge and an anchor; for those at a crossroads, it will steady your soul. This book won't just fuel your fire—it will remind you why you lit the flame."

—Ben Crump, Renowned Civil Rights Attorney and *Time* 100 Most Influential People in the World Honoree

"Michael Leach effortlessly navigates what it means to constantly climb over hurdles of adversity and provides you with the GPS map to find that same tenacity within your own heart. His words are sharp, timely, and necessary for the culture."

—Roy Wood Jr., Host of CNN's *Have I Got News for You* and Former Correspondent for *The Daily Show*

"Nobody can read Michael Leach's story and not be inspired. It is one of grit, commitment, and determination to overcome challenges and to make uncertainty an ally. Michael has grown into a leader whose voice is respected far beyond the playing field. *Faith Over Fear* shows how he did it. More important, it tells you how you can do it as well."

—Jeff Pash, Executive Vice President and General Counsel, National Football League

"I gave Michael his first shot in the NFL—and I've watched him walk through doors few expected him to enter, always with humility, faith, and discipline. *Faith Over Fear* doesn't just tell a good story; it equips anyone facing uncertainty with the strength, strategy, and conviction this moment demands. In times like these, we need every word."

—Lovie Smith, NFL Head Coach, 2005 NFL Coach of the Year, and Texas Sports Hall of Fame Inductee

"*Faith Over Fear* offers a compelling framework for leading with clarity and conviction in uncertain times. Michael Leach's story bridges personal experience with universal insight, reminding us that real impact is built through courage, conscience, and purpose. This is a timely and resonant contribution."

—Charles H. Rivkin, Chairman and CEO of the Motion Picture Association (MPA)

"This book carries the fire of lived experience and the breath of the Holy Spirit. *Faith Over Fear* is not just Michael's story—it's a roadmap for every believer called to lead when the path isn't clear. Bold, Spirit-filled, and right on time."

—Dr. Rich Wilkerson Sr. and Dr. Robyn Wilkerson, Founders of Peacemakers and Senior Pastors of Trinity Legacy Center (Miami, Florida)

"*Faith Over Fear* is a powerful story of resilience, ambition, and hope. At once humble and determined, self-reflective and bold, Michael's journey rises above the personal to offer a profound meditation on a nation still striving to fulfill its stated ideals. With the voice of a natural storyteller and a deep sense of history, he reminds us that what we do now matters—and that real courage is found in the choices we make in our own time to forge a better tomorrow."

—Kim Sajet, First Woman to Serve as Director of the Smithsonian National Portrait Gallery and Art Historian

"*Faith Over Fear* is more than a book—it's a blueprint. For leaders who've stood on the shoulders of giants while carrying legacies forward, Michael's story offers both a mirror for reflection and a roadmap for action. Rooted in truth, charged with purpose, and anchored in possibility, this is required reading for every leader from every walk of life—building on the promises of yesterday by building a tomorrow with equal parts of care, courage, and conviction."

—Dr. Sesha Joi Moon, Chief Impact Officer for Girl Scouts of the USA and Former Chief Diversity Officer of the US House of Representatives for the 117th & 118th Congresses

"*Faith Over Fear* is for anyone who's ever been underestimated, counted out, or told to wait their turn—but kept going anyway.

It's for those who believed in a better future before it was visible. This book is the spark so many of us have been waiting for. After you read it, you'll know why."

—Cristóbal Alex, Chairman of the Board of the Latino Victory Fund and Former White House Deputy Cabinet Secretary

"*Faith Over Fear* is a testament to perseverance, purpose, hope, and the power of community. Michael's journey speaks to the resilience we carry, the battles we fight, and the future we're building—together. This book is a gift that will stay with you and ignite the courage to build what's never been built before."

—Sindy Benavides, Founding Executive Director of Aquí: The Accountability Movement and Former CEO of the League of United Latin American Citizens (LULAC)

"*Faith Over Fear* is a masterclass in courageous leadership. Michael Leach invites us to reject performative progress and instead lead with vision, values, and conviction. This book isn't just timely— it's necessary. Every boardroom, classroom, and family table should be talking about what's in these pages."

— Jocelyn Moore, Board Director of DraftKings, OppFi, and First Responder Network Authority; Former NFL Executive Vice President; and Tony-Nominated Producer

Faith
Over
Fear

Harnessing Resilience
in the Face *of* Uncertainty

———

MICHAEL LEACH

HarperOne
An Imprint of HarperCollins*Publishers*

HarperCollins books may be purchased for educational, business, or sales promotional use. For information, please email the Special Markets Department at SPsales@harpercollins.com.

harpercollins.com

FIRST EDITION

Designed by Yvonne Chan

Library of Congress Cataloging-in-Publication Data has been applied for.

ISBN 978-0-06-344296-2

25 26 27 28 29 LBC 5 4 3 2 1

To God the Father, Jesus Christ the Son, and the Holy Spirit—
my source of faith, hope, and love.

To my wife, Brittany, and our twin daughters, Lela and Nia—
your love, light, and unwavering support inspire me and
remind me daily of what truly matters.

To my parents, Mitchell and Maria Leach,
for laying the foundation of faith that I continue to walk upon.

Contents

Faith Over Fear—
The Gap We Must Close

WHAT DRIVES US FORWARD? IS IT THE PURSUIT OF OUR ideals—those lofty visions we hold for ourselves and for the world? Or is it something deeper, something rooted in the tension between who we are and who we could become? As you open this book, I want to take you on a journey—a journey not just through my life but through the many universal themes we all wrestle with, individually and collectively.

This is an exploration of faith and fear, of ideals and realities. It's about the gap that exists between what we aspire to and what we often settle for, both as individuals and as a society. In many ways, this gap is a defining feature of the human experience. We live in the space between our hopes and our limitations, between the promises we cling to and the obstacles that seem insurmountable.

That tension has never felt more urgent than it does today. I am writing this at a time of profound transition—when long-standing institutions, once seen as immovable, are undergoing dramatic shifts. Across industries and government, organizations are being restructured, agencies are being downsized, and entire departments are being dissolved in the name of efficiency and cost cutting. The result? Thousands of public servants and private-sector employees finding themselves suddenly without jobs, entire divisions of government and business being reshaped or eliminated, and critical social programs facing uncertain futures.

The impact of these changes is being felt in every corner of society. The US Agency for International Development (USAID), which once employed more than ten thousand individuals dedicated to humanitarian efforts worldwide, has been reduced to nearly three hundred, a fraction of its existing workforce, altering the scope of its global mission. The Department of Justice has seen an unprecedented number of resignations from senior officials navigating shifts in legal priorities. The Centers for Disease Control and Prevention (CDC), long relied upon for public health guidance, has had its communication channels restricted, altering how it engages with the public. Meanwhile, an unprecedented number of federal jobs have been eliminated, leaving agencies to reassess how they fulfill their missions with fewer resources.

Beyond the public sector, private companies are adjusting to new pressures as well. Many corporations have scaled back or dissolved long-standing diversity, equity, and inclusion (DEI) initiatives, reversing years of progress in creating more equitable and inclusive workplaces. Even the National Park Service, which safeguards some of America's most revered natural spaces, has been impacted with staffing reductions limiting operational capacity at sites across the country.

At the same time, larger constitutional discussions are taking shape, with debates emerging over issues like birthright citizenship—raising fundamental questions about national identity, law, and the evolving definition of American rights and freedoms.

These shifts aren't just headlines; they are real-life disruptions that shape communities, livelihoods, and the collective landscape of opportunity. They highlight the reality that change—whether welcomed or resisted—can be unsettling, and the uncertainty it brings can test our faith in what comes next. But uncertainty isn't new.

By the time this book is released into the world, nearly two years—almost to the day—will have passed since I left the White House—two years of reflection, growth, and witnessing firsthand how quickly the world can change. The timing feels significant, not just for me but for all of us. Because if the past few years have shown us anything, it's that history moves fast, and moments of transition—whether personal or national—have a way of testing who we are and what we truly believe in.

At every major inflection point in history, individuals, institutions, and nations have had to navigate moments like this—moments when the future felt unclear, when the path forward seemed uncertain, and when the weight of transition made people question whether progress was still possible. The challenge we face is not just in understanding these changes but in deciding how we respond to them.

History has shown us that these moments, though unsettling, are not new. And yet, we've been here before.

My journey—from the NFL to the White House, from the streets of Chicago to the halls of power—has been shaped by this very tension. I've wrestled with it personally, and I've witnessed it on a national stage. Along the way, I've learned that the choice we make between faith and fear is not just a personal one—it's a decision that shapes the world around us.

The roles I've held led me to realize one undeniable truth: Our greatest challenges and opportunities often come down to whether we choose to close the gap between our ideals and our realities.

Faith Over Fear isn't just my story—it's your story, too. Each of us, in our own way, stands at the crossroads of faith and fear. Our circumstances may be different, but I know you've faced moments where fear tried to dictate your decisions, where doubt whispered in your ear and made you question whether you could take that next step. That's what this book is about—recognizing those moments and choosing to move forward in faith, despite the fear.

As a society, we're constantly grappling with the gap between the ideals we hold up—liberty, justice, equality—and the realities we live in. Whether it's the struggle for racial equity, the division we see in our political landscape, or the personal battles we face in our own lives, the challenge remains the same: How do we close the gap?

In America, this question is as old as the nation itself. We were founded on ideals that promised freedom and opportunity for all, but the reality has often been far more complicated. I'll show you how this tension between ideals and realities has played out in my life and in the larger story of our country. More important, I'll offer insights and principles that will help you close that gap in your own life—whether you're navigating your career, relationships, personal growth, or even the complex social challenges we all face as citizens.

You may be wondering why my story matters. It matters because I know what it's like to stand in the gap between where you are and where you hope to be—to feel the weight of uncertainty and wonder if the path ahead is even possible. But it also matters because the questions I'm going to answer in this book aren't just about me—they're about you. The lessons I've learned, the setbacks I've overcome, and the principles I'll share aren't just my own—they belong to anyone seeking clarity, courage, and the wisdom to navigate whatever stands before them, knowing that each choice is shaping them into who they are truly meant to become.

No matter who you are or where you find yourself in life, we all share in the power of choice. We may not choose where we are born or the circumstances we inherit, but the decisions we make—especially when it comes to faith or fear—define everything that follows. As you'll see throughout this book, those choices have the power to shape not just our own lives but the world around us.

As a young Black man from the South Side of Chicago, I had to learn early how to navigate the world with both hope and resilience. I've been in rooms where decisions that affect millions of lives are made, and I've seen how fear—whether personal or systemic—can paralyze even the most powerful among us. I've also seen what happens when faith moves us forward.

That's why I wrote this book. Because I've seen firsthand the incredible things that can happen when we choose faith—when we decide to step into the unknown, trusting that the path forward will be revealed as we walk it.

My hope is that you'll see yourself in these pages. Whether you're standing on the cusp of a major life decision or simply reflecting on your own path, the themes of this book are universal. We all have moments where fear and faith collide, and we all have the power to choose which one will shape our future.

I invite you to walk with me on this journey. Together, we'll explore what it means to close the gap between our ideals and our realities—not just for ourselves, but for the world around us. This isn't just about survival; it's about thriving. It's about understanding that the choices we make today will define the lives we lead tomorrow. And it's about choosing, in every moment, to walk in faith rather than fear.

Part I
Choices That Make Us

CHAPTER 1

My NFL Origins

I STOOD AT MIDFIELD OF SOLDIER FIELD, HOME TO THE CHI-cago Bears—my hometown team—feeling the rumble of a billion-dollar empire beneath my feet. In that moment, one truth hit me hard: Faith and fear both ask the same of you—to believe in something that hasn't happened yet. The only difference? Which one you choose to follow. Growing up on the South Side of Chicago, I learned early that life doesn't hand out guarantees—it offers chances, often disguised as risks. I've faced the crossroads of fear and faith more times than I can count. And in every pivotal moment, one truth has always been clear: While fear offers safety, faith promises transformation.

Here's the question I keep coming back to: When the stakes are sky-high, when everything you've worked for could fall apart in an instant, what bridges the gap between your ideals and the stark reality staring you in the face? As I transitioned from the gridiron to the White House, one realization hit hard: Choosing fear is easy—it offers the illusion of control. Choosing faith is where the real transformation happens. Faith doesn't just connect us to our aspirations; it empowers us to turn those aspirations into something real, something lasting.

That question—ultimately about the tension between fear and faith—wasn't new. It had shaped my journey from the very beginning.

Born in the late '80s to parents Mitchell and Maria Leach, I came from a middle-class upbringing deeply rooted in faith. My story is one of pursuing the ideals I aspired to and confronting the realities I faced, a journey where faith continually bridged the gap between what was and what could be.

How did a young Black boy from Chicago navigate a world that often seems indifferent to his existence? How did he balance his dreams with the harsh realities of the world around him?

For as long as I can remember, from the age of three through adulthood, I admired how it felt to be dressed in a professional suit, like a "businessman," as I used to call it. To be perceived as a businessman—someone important, admired, and approachable—was a feeling or a thought I found myself drawn to in my early years. Perhaps this masked deeper fears of being seen as unadmirable, unimportant, or unintelligent—only time would tell.

Growing up in a predominantly Black neighborhood, our financial limitations were not something I was acutely aware of as a child. What I did know, though, was that the world outside my front door came with invisible boundaries, boundaries my parents were adamant I respected. I wasn't allowed to ride my bike freely through the neighborhood like some kids. Instead, my rides were confined to a short stretch of sidewalk.

Every day, I'd walk my bike out of the house and mount it on the sidewalk directly in front of our home. From there, I could ride only as far as the second-to-last house on our block. Once I reached that invisible line, I'd stop, turn the bike around, and head back in the other direction, but only until I reached the second-to-last house on the other side. Back and forth, back and forth. I wasn't permitted to cross the street and ride on the sidewalk on the other side. That was the world my parents allowed me to navigate—a stretch of concrete that was both a source of freedom and a reminder of the dangers they never fully explained.

Looking back, I now understand what my parents were trying to protect me from. Those limits were put in place because of the very real dangers that existed beyond that second-to-last house— potential gang activity, drug dealings, violence. As a child, I didn't see the full scope of it. But my parents did, and they made sure the boundaries of my world kept me safe.

But here's the irony: The very rules meant to protect us often end up shaping the boundaries we impose on ourselves. Those bike rides taught me more than just the importance of safety—they showed me that the limitations we inherit often stay with us long after we've outgrown them.

While some boundaries were meant to protect us from external dangers, my parents made sure there were others that grounded us in something greater—faith, hope, and love. Faith wasn't just something my parents taught; it was something they lived. Our family attended Faith Tabernacle, a small Baptist church nestled in the heart of Chicago. Like many predominantly Black Baptist churches, the services weren't bound by time—they were measured in spirit. Hours would pass as the congregation sang, prayed, and worshipped with fervor. As a young boy, I often dreaded the length of those services. I'd sneak Sweetarts or Starburst candies into my pocket to keep me occupied, a tiny act that helped me pass the time. But even in my youthful impatience, I couldn't ignore the deep sense of community and purpose that filled the sanctuary.

My parents were devout but not in a way that felt burdensome or ritualistic. While others might have labeled them "religious," I've come to see it differently. Religion, to me, is a set of rules and obligations—something done for God out of duty. What my parents demonstrated was something far deeper: a relationship with God, one that permeated every aspect of their lives and ours.

They didn't just pray; they lived their prayers. They encouraged me and my two brothers to involve God in our daily decisions, no matter how small. Every meal began with grace, every morning started with a prayer before we left for school, and every evening ended with a sacred family ritual. We would gather around our well-worn *Daily Word* devotional book, a staple in our household. Each night, one of us would take turns reading the day's passage—a short blurb beginning with a Bible verse, followed by a thoughtful reflection, and ending with a prayer. These moments weren't grand or performative; they were intimate, a way of grounding us in faith amid the noise of life.

Their relationship with God wasn't confined to the walls of a church. On Christmas, instead of basking in the warmth of our own celebrations, my parents would pack us into the car with gifts they had purchased—books, toys, or other small treasures. As a family, we'd visit a nearby hospital to hand-deliver those gifts to children spending the holidays away from home. We didn't belong to an organization or a group; it wasn't part of some public outreach effort. It was just us. Quiet, intentional, and profoundly personal.

It was through these actions—these unspoken lessons—that my parents taught me what it meant to live like Jesus. Their faith wasn't a checklist; it was a way of being. They wanted us to understand that faith wasn't about what we said but how we lived and that our lives could be a testament to God's love.

> *Faith wasn't about what we said but how we lived.*

This foundation of faith shaped so much of who I am, and it's why certain traditions stand out so vividly in my memory.

One holiday that stood out to me was New Year's Eve. Unlike many who celebrate with fireworks and gatherings, our family had a different tradition—a tradition born out of necessity and faith. As the final hours of the year ticked away, my parents, my two brothers, and I would turn off all the lights in the house and gather in my parents' bedroom to pray through the night. We didn't just pray out of religious duty; we prayed for protection and for hope— hope for something better in the year to come.

My parents explained that people in our neighborhood would shoot firearms into the air to celebrate, and they feared that stray bullets might hit homes with illuminated lights. For my family, survival was in the small things—like the simple act of turning off a light to keep the danger from noticing us. We weren't just celebrating the arrival of a new year; we were praying to see the next one.

I would sit there in the darkness, my small hands clasped together, repeating the same prayer over and over again: "God, bless us with a new house, a big backyard with a swimming pool, a safe neighborhood, and a job that would let me change the world." Even as a child, my prayers weren't just about the present; they were about the future. I wasn't only asking for a better life; I was praying for the life I dreamed of, the one that seemed so far out of reach on those long, dark nights. And yet, deep down, I believed that it could happen. That's the thing about faith—you believe in the unseen, even when everything around you says it's impossible.

And then, one day, it happened.

I was nine years old when we left the South Side of Chicago and moved to the South Suburbs, to a place called Richton Park. My older brother was fourteen, my younger brother just five. This move symbolized something deeper than a change of address—it represented hope, a step closer to the life my parents had envisioned for us.

Athletics were a cornerstone of our upbringing. My parents always kept us involved in sports, from park district leagues and YMCA teams to AAU basketball programs. I played basketball, football, track and field, baseball, soccer—if it involved competition and teamwork, I was in. But one lesson from that period stands out more than any other.

As a young boy, I was captivated by the Power Rangers and their gravity-defying flips. I begged my parents to let me learn how to do flips like the Power Rangers. To my surprise, they signed me up for a gymnastics program at our local park district. On the first day, I walked into the gym with my head held high, ready to conquer the flips I'd seen on TV. But as I looked around, my excitement turned to dread. I was the only boy in the entire class. My shyness and the unexpected circumstances made me feel out of place. After the second session, I begged my parents to unenroll me. I pleaded for them to let me quit.

But their response was firm: "You have to finish what you start." They wouldn't let me give up just because the situation wasn't what I'd expected. It wasn't about the money they'd already spent; it was about the principle. They believed in the adage, "You can't finish what you don't start, and you should never start what you're not committed to finishing." Begrudgingly, I stuck it out and completed the program. What I didn't realize at the time was that this lesson—about perseverance, commitment, and seeing things through—would shape so much of who I would become later in life.

Amid the midnight prayers, the move from Chicago, and that humbling gymnastics class, sports remained my passion. Growing up in Chicago during the heyday of the Bulls dynasty, my brothers and I idolized Michael Jordan, Scottie Pippen, and B. J. Armstrong. "I wanna be like Mike" wasn't just a catchy jingle—it was a mantra for kids like us. We'd spend hours pretending to be our favorite Bulls players, shooting hoops in the driveway or at the park. My older brother, as the eldest, claimed the coveted role of Jordan. I, much to my disappointment, had to settle for Pippen, and my younger brother proudly played the part of Armstrong.

We even went so far as to make our own Bulls jerseys. My mom took us to a craft store, where we picked out iron-on letters and numbers to create makeshift jerseys from thrift-store tank tops. They weren't official gear, but to us, they might as well have been championship rings. Wearing those homemade jerseys, we didn't just dream about playing for the Bulls—we believed we could.

For years, I thought sports would be my path, my way of making something of myself. I played on teams year after year, honing my skills and holding on to that dream of "going pro." But as much as I loved the game and poured my heart into it, reality had other plans.

The first real challenge of my journey came with a harsh realization: Despite my newfound freedom, my athletic abilities wouldn't carry me to the future I had imagined. I didn't make the varsity basketball or football teams in high school. In a community where "going pro" was often seen as one of the few golden tickets out, that hit hard. Up until that point, my vision for my future was centered around becoming a professional athlete—something almost every young Black boy in my community aspired to.

> *If I wasn't good enough to excel in sports, then what was I good enough for?*

That rejection was more than just a missed opportunity, it was a confrontation with a harsh reality: I wasn't good enough, at least not in the ways that I thought mattered. My body couldn't keep up with the dreams I had for it, and that left me feeling hollow, unworthy. In the eyes of my community, sports were one of the most visible ways to achieve success. If I wasn't good enough to excel in that, then what was I good enough for?

In those early days of high school, rejection weighed heavily on me. As my friends made the varsity teams, I found myself sitting on the sidelines, questioning my place in a world where athletic success seemed like the way out. There's something about being left out that forces you to confront the reality of your own limitations, and at that age, it felt like the world was telling me I didn't measure up.

But sometimes, when one door closes, another one opens in the most unexpected way. My older brother, Mitchell, saw my struggle, and in his quiet, yet impactful way, he offered a different perspective. "Why not combine your love for sports with business?" he suggested, planting the seed that would grow into something far greater than I could have imagined. At the time, sports management wasn't something I'd seriously considered, but the more I thought about it, the more sense it made.

It's a strange thing—how a single conversation can completely change the trajectory of your life. Looking back, that one suggestion from my brother was the spark that set me on a new path. Sometimes we think we know exactly where we're headed, only to be gently nudged in a direction we hadn't considered. And often, those nudges come from the people closest to us.

When it was time to apply to colleges, I walked into the guidance counselor's office full of hope and excitement, ready to take the next step toward my future. But Ms. Lawson, my high school counselor, quickly brought me down from my lofty ambitions. With a few words, she cast doubt on my potential, saying, "You're not going to get into the University of Illinois at Urbana-Champaign." My ACT scores weren't up to par with other applicants who had been accepted in the past.

The words stung. For a moment, it felt like my dreams were slipping away before I even had the chance to chase them. The University of Illinois had been my top choice—an institution where I saw myself thriving, growing, and making a name for my-self. But in that instant, it seemed like the door was being closed on me, just like it had been with sports.

What happens when someone in a position of authority tells you that you're not good enough? That's the question I wrestled with as I walked out of her office, a knot forming in my stomach. It wasn't just about the rejection; it was about being told, in no uncertain terms, that I didn't belong. For a young Black man from Chicago, those words carry a weight that's hard to describe. It's as if the system itself is reinforcing every doubt you've ever had about whether you're truly capable of achieving greatness.

Here's where the story shifts. In moments like this, when fear and doubt threaten to consume you, there's often someone in your corner—someone whose faith in you is greater than your own. For me, that person was my mother. She refused to let those doubts take root. "God has a plan to use all parts of you to reach your potential," she told me, her voice firm but loving. "Not just some parts, all parts."

Her words did something to me. They reignited a flame that had been flickering, reminding me that my journey wasn't dictated by a counselor's assessment. It was dictated by something much greater—faith. This was my first real lesson in choosing faith over fear. Fear would have told me to accept the limits placed on me. But faith? Faith asked me to believe in a version of myself that others couldn't yet see.

How many of us have let someone else's doubt become our truth? How often have we allowed a single opinion to shape our reality? What I've learned through this experience—and countless others—is that the story someone tells you about your limitations isn't the story you have to live by.

My mother's faith became the bridge between my fear and my future. Had I listened to my guidance counselor, I might have never applied to the University of Illinois. I might have taken the "safer" route, the one she thought I was capable of, instead of aiming for the stars. I pushed forward because of my mother's unwavering belief in me. And here's the irony: I was accepted.

Acceptance into the University of Illinois wasn't just about being admitted into a prestigious school, it was a turning point. It was a reminder that faith, coupled with action, can overcome even the most daunting obstacles. This moment, this victory, became a defining chapter in my story.

It wasn't just my victory—it was a victory for all the young people who have been told they're not enough. It was a victory for anyone who has ever had their potential dismissed by someone who couldn't see the full scope of their dreams. It's a reminder that no one holds the final word on your future except you and God. People can misjudge your potential because they're only looking at the chapter you're in now, but they don't hold the pen to your story. Never let someone else's limited vision become the limit of your ambition.

Years later, after achieving success in the NFL, I was invited back to my high school to deliver a motivational speech to the students. The irony of that moment wasn't lost on me. There I was, standing in the very same hallways where my dreams had once been doubted, now speaking to a room full of students about the power of perseverance. And wouldn't you know it? My old guidance counselor was there. So was the basketball coach who cut me after my first tryout. Life has a way of coming full circle, doesn't it?

Arriving at the University of Illinois was like stepping into a whole new world. On the surface, it seemed like the culmination of everything I had worked for—a prestigious university, a chance to rewrite my future. But underneath the excitement was the harsh reality: navigating this space as a young Black man wasn't going to be easy.

Move-in day felt like the beginning of a new chapter. The campus, vast and beautiful, held the promise of academic success, new friendships, and the pursuit of what people so often call "the American Dream." But something didn't sit right with me as we unloaded the car at Florida Avenue Residence Hall, known to students as FAR.

There's something about seeing a large number of Black students moving into the same dorm that forces you to ask uncomfortable questions. It was surprising, even disorienting. A friend from high school had told me the University of Illinois was predominantly white, so I expected a different experience. But FAR, tucked away on the southeastern edge of the campus, felt to me like an enclave—it seemed to create an unspoken distance between many of the Black students and the rest of the university. It was the first time I began to question the idea of "inclusion" in a space that boasted diversity but seemed to struggle with integration. And then there was the distance both literal and symbolic. Every day, the bus ride from FAR to the Quad, the central hub of campus life, felt like a journey across invisible boundaries. As I boarded the bus at FAR, the majority of faces were Black, but as we approached the main campus, the demographic shifted dramatically. By the time we reached the Quad, I was often one of the few Black students in sight. That commute was a constant reminder of the social distance between where I was and where I wanted to be. It was as though we had been placed on the periphery, both literally and figuratively, making it clear that while we were part of the university, we weren't truly integrated into its fabric.

Think about this: How many of us, especially those from marginalized communities, have experienced this same feeling? Being present but not fully seen, included but not truly integrated? The distance from FAR to the Quad mirrored the distance I felt from the ideal of belonging in a predominantly white institution.

In Fall 2005, the University of Illinois had a total enrollment of nearly forty-two thousand students. Of those, only about 6 percent were Black. The contrast between the ideal of attending a prestigious university and the reality of navigating a predominantly white space quickly became apparent. I began to wonder if this was just the beginning. Would this experience mirror what I'd face in the professional world? Would I always be navigating spaces where I was one of the few people of color, constantly balancing the ideals I aspired to with the realities that seemed to challenge my very presence?

These questions weighed heavily on me as I tried to find my place on campus. Socially, it was a challenge to integrate, and academically, the rigor of the coursework presented its own hurdles. I was determined to carve out a space for myself, even if it meant navigating two worlds—one that expected me to assimilate and another that constantly reminded me I was different.

It was through my intentional involvement in the Illini Union Board that I found a sense of belonging and purpose. The Illini Union Board is the student-run organization responsible for programming many of the university's key events—events designed to engage, inspire, and unite students from all walks of life. During the second semester of my freshman year, I had the unexpected privilege of becoming the area director for traditional programs, a role typically held by upper-level students. The senior who preceded me saw something in me—potential, drive, or maybe even faith—and believed I was the right person to lead, despite my age. In this role, I oversaw a series of campus events, including African American homecoming initiatives, the Mother's Day fashion show, and the dads' day program.

Being entrusted with this role was significant. Not only had I gone through an extensive interview process, but stepping into this position marked my first real exposure to leading initiatives that focused on ensuring underrepresented groups—especially the African American student population—felt seen, heard, and valued. In many ways, this was a positive reflection of the university's commitment to diversity and inclusion. They could have ignored the need for such programming, but instead, they invested in it. It was a realization that while the university had its challenges, it was also taking steps to acknowledge and address the complexities of student life for people of color.

This experience was not just about organizing events; it was about ensuring that people like me had a space to feel celebrated. It was about being a part of something bigger than myself, using my voice to uplift a community I was a part of. Looking back, this may have been the first time I stepped into a leadership role where my purpose aligned with making sure an underrepresented group felt seen and valued. It planted a seed, one that would grow into a lifelong commitment to advocating for inclusivity and representation in spaces where it was often lacking.

Yes, the reality of navigating a predominantly white institution was difficult, but there were also moments of growth, connection, and progress. My involvement with the Illini Union Board was one of those moments. It balanced out the isolation I felt in other areas and gave me a sense of belonging. It was a reminder that even in the face of challenges, there are opportunities to contribute to something meaningful, to shape the world around you.

But then came another turning point. Amid the challenges and triumphs of finding my place, something happened that shifted my perspective entirely.

During my freshman year, while I was working on an assignment in the FAR computer lab, I struck up a conversation with another student sitting next to me. We bonded quickly over our shared interest in sports, and he mentioned something that struck a chord: He had written a letter to the head coach of the Illinois men's basketball team, asking for a position as a student manager. His initiative left a mark on me. Here was someone who wasn't waiting for opportunity to knock, he was building his own door. I realized in that moment that while I had spent so much time trying to navigate the social and academic complexities of college life, I hadn't been as intentional about securing a role in the athletic programs—something I had always envisioned for myself. I had come to this university with dreams of being involved in sports, but so far, I hadn't taken any concrete steps to make that happen.

This conversation shifted something in me. I couldn't afford to be passive. If I wanted to carve out a future in sports management, I needed to take action. I began relentlessly pursuing opportunities within the athletic department. I sent emails, made phone calls, and wrote letters to various people in the intercollegiate athletics department, hoping that someone would give me a chance. And then one day, opportunity knocked. I noticed a flyer inside the elevator of my dorm advertising a men's basketball team watch party for an upcoming game against a Big Ten rival. The flyer mentioned that the event was designed to help foster community and belonging among underrepresented students, with transportation provided for those living in dorms farther from the event, like FAR. But what really caught my attention was the fact that staff members, coaches, and other personnel from the athletic department would be in attendance.

How many times in life do we overlook the small opportunities that could lead to something bigger? That flyer could have easily been dismissed as just another campus event; a social gathering meant for casual fun. I saw something more—a chance to make a meaningful connection with the people who could open doors for me in the world of sports. While most of my classmates donned their best Illini gear for the watch party, I took a different approach. I spent time in the computer lab printing copies of my résumé and dressed in slacks and a button-down shirt. To some, it may have seemed overkill—after all, it was just a basketball watch party—but for me, it was an opportunity to show that I was serious about my future. My classmates joked about my formal attire, but I knew this was more than just attending a game. This was about positioning myself for the future I wanted.

At the watch party, I met Cassie Arner, the woman in charge of communications and public relations for the Illini football team. We struck up a conversation, and I shared my aspirations of working in sports management. Cassie was kind enough to introduce me to several staff members, including Mike Locksley, one of the coaches on the football team. Coach Locksley encouraged me to follow up with him after the event, and that follow-up would prove to be one of the most pivotal moments in my college career.

The doors started to open. By the second semester of my freshman year, I was offered a position as a student manager for the Illinois football team under Head Coach Ron Zook. This was more than just a part-time job for me; it was a foot in the door, the first real step toward achieving my dreams. I threw myself into the work with enthusiasm, determined to prove myself and make the most of the opportunity.

This was a clear demonstration of how faith in action can bridge the gap between ideals and reality. It was a reminder that success doesn't just come from believing in what's possible; it comes from actively pursuing it, from taking the steps that others might be hesitant to take. It's easy to look back and connect the dots, to see how one small decision led to a bigger opportunity. In the moment, it doesn't always feel that way. Sometimes we have to take risks, not knowing how they'll pan out, trusting that faith will guide us through the uncertainty.

This period of my life taught me another valuable lesson: It's not just about who you know, but who knows you and what you stand for. In an industry as competitive as sports, relationships are key. It's not enough to just be in the room, you have to make your presence known. You have to show people not only what you're capable of but what you believe in, what drives you. That watch party wasn't just an event. It was a moment that allowed me to step into a bigger story, one that would lead to more opportunities down the road. Working as a student manager gave me insights into the inner workings of a Division I football team. I learned about the operations of the sport in addition to leadership, discipline, and the importance of staying ready for when the next opportunity presents itself.

The question is: How often do we hesitate to take the steps that could change everything? How often do we let fear of rejection or failure keep us from pursuing what we truly want? And more important, what happens when we choose faith over fear? What happens when we decide to show up, even when the odds seem stacked against us?

Now, let's zoom out for a moment. What happens when we think about this concept of faith versus fear in the context of society as a whole? The tension between ideals and realities isn't just an individual struggle—it's a collective one. And just like in our personal journeys, the choice to act in faith, to pursue progress even in the face of uncertainty, is what drives transformation.

As I reflect on that period of my life, from taking that initial step into the world of sports management to navigating the complexities of balancing academics, social life, and professional aspirations, I realize that it wasn't just about me. It was about the bigger picture—about how we all navigate the tensions between our ideals and the realities we face. Whether we're talking about individuals, communities, or entire nations, the questions remain the same: Will we choose fear, or will we choose faith? Will we let the obstacles and challenges of today keep us from pursuing the possibilities of tomorrow?

As the weeks and months passed, I found myself increasingly involved in my role as a student manager for the Illinois football team. It wasn't just a job; it was an education in leadership, perseverance, and what it takes to operate at the highest levels of collegiate sports. The long hours, the grueling practices, the meticulous attention to detail weren't just aspects of the job; they were life lessons in disguise. Later a defining opportunity to intern with the Chicago Bears presented itself, and this set the stage for everything that followed. I had dreamed of working with an NFL team for years. And yet, as exciting as the opportunity was, it didn't come easily. It required persistence, relationship-building, and a fair amount of faith.

My brother Mitchell played a key role in this dream. He had worked in sports broadcasting and had a connection within the Bears' advertising and events department. Mitchell introduced me to someone on the Bears' staff, and from there, I took the reins. I built rapport, nurtured the relationship over time, and kept my foot in the door, hoping that when the moment presented itself, I'd be ready.

That opportunity was a four-week internship during the Bears' 2007 training camp. It was the kind of experience I knew could shape the course of my career. But there's something important to understand here: Opportunities like this don't just fall into your lap. They require preparation, persistence, and yes, a leap of faith. I had no guarantees that this internship would lead to anything more, but I knew that I had to make the most of it. So, I threw myself into the internship with everything I had. My goal was simple: to meet as many people as possible and to make a lasting impression. Day after day, I sought out staffers, coaches, and anyone who would take a moment to talk to me. While some, like the Bears' head equipment manager and a few others, shared quick pleasantries with me, most couldn't sit down for deeper conversations. The fast-paced and demanding nature of an NFL training camp meant that time was scarce, especially for senior leaders. In many ways, it was a matter of both hierarchy and availability—it's not typical for leaders at this level to carve out time for an intern during such a high-stakes, high-pressure season. I began to understand that connecting meaningfully in this setting would require persistence—and perhaps patience. I shadowed team operations, learned the intricate details of event planning, and absorbed the NFL culture. The experience was exhilarating and unlike anything I had experienced before. However, as the end of the internship approached, I felt a nagging sense of disappointment. Despite all my efforts, none of the key Bears staff members I had hoped to connect with sat down to have a conversation with me. I worried that my internship would end without the valuable connections I had hoped to make. And then, on the last day of my internship, something unexpected happened.

I was leaving the cafeteria after lunch, feeling both full and slightly dejected, when I bumped into Andrew Hayes-Stoker, the Bears' football operations assistant. He was one of the key people I had been trying to meet throughout my internship. Fate—or perhaps divine intervention—had placed him right in front of me at that exact moment.

Before I could even apologize for nearly running into him, he smiled and asked, "Hey, do you have time for dinner?"

Despite having just finished a meal, I didn't hesitate. I quickly grabbed another tray and joined him at a nearby table. This was the moment I had been waiting for—the chance to connect with someone who could open doors for me. What followed wasn't just a casual conversation. It was an opportunity to glean wisdom from someone who had been navigating the world of professional sports for years.

Andrew shared his journey through the coaching ranks, his experiences with the Bears, and the lessons he had learned along the way. His story wasn't just about the NFL; it was about resilience, perseverance, and the importance of staying ready for when opportunity knocks. But one piece of advice stood out more than any other. Andrew told me, "It's not just about who you know; it's about who knows you and what you stand for. Always make sure people know what you're about."

That statement became a guiding principle in my life from that day forward. It wasn't enough to simply know people in the industry—I needed to make sure that the people who mattered knew who I was and what I stood for. It was about building a reputation, about being someone people could trust and depend on.

That conversation with Andrew was more than just a meeting. It was a pivotal moment in my journey—a reminder that sometimes the most meaningful connections come when you least expect them. But it's also a reminder of the importance of faith. Had I not been ready to seize that moment, I might have walked away from my internship without making the connection that would propel me forward. As I look back on that experience, I realize that faith isn't just about believing in what's possible—it's about staying ready for the moment when possibility becomes reality. It's about putting yourself in the right positions, even when you're not sure how things will turn out. And it's about trusting that, when the time comes, you'll be ready to step through the door. Faith isn't passive—it's active. It's about doing your part while trusting God to do His. Growing up, my parents often reminded me of 2 Corinthians 5:7 (NKJV): "For we walk by faith, not by sight." That trust shaped how I approached every challenge, including that internship. I had been walking by faith every single day, trusting that my efforts weren't in vain. While I couldn't see Andrew waiting on the other side of that door, God could. When I think about doors—whether they're literal like the one I opened that led me to Andrew or metaphorical like the opportunities I've prayed for—I'm reminded of this: You're just one person away, one conversation away, or one moment of courage away from stepping into a new season of your life. It's preparation and action that turn those moments into opportunities.

How many of us have found ourselves at the end of an opportunity feeling like we missed out on what we were really hoping for? How often do we walk away from an experience thinking that it wasn't what we expected, only to realize later that we had everything we needed all along? Sometimes the lessons we learn, the relationships we build, and the experiences we gather aren't immediately clear. It's only with time, reflection, and faith that we see how all the pieces fit together.

Returning to campus after my internship, I felt a mix of emotions. On one hand, I was grateful for the experience and the connections I had made. On the other hand, I knew there was still so much more to learn. Something had shifted in me during that summer with the Bears. I saw what was possible, and I knew that I wanted more. I wanted to be part of something bigger, to continue learning and growing, and to keep pushing myself beyond the imaginable.

Just a week after my internship with the Bears concluded, I received a phone call that would change the trajectory of my fall semester. Matt, the head of the Bears' advertising and events team, reached out to tell me how impressed they were with my performance during training camp. He offered me an opportunity to join their game-day staff for the upcoming regular season. This wasn't just any offer—it was an invitation to work with the Bears' advertising and events team, supporting critical elements of game-day operations at Soldier Field. The role itself wasn't glamorous, but it was pivotal. I'd be responsible for tasks ranging from setting up corporate sales displays and supporting advertising partner activations around the stadium to managing logistics for the Bears' drumline and facilitating pregame player introductions. It was hands-on work that required precision, adaptability, and a willingness to embrace the chaos of NFL game days. The season would run from September through December 2007, and I saw it as an invaluable chance to deepen my connections within the organization and prove that I was ready for bigger opportunities in the future.

But with the offer came significant challenges. Balancing a full course load, my commitments to the Illinois football team, and this new opportunity wasn't going to be easy. And then, there was another layer of complexity—a decision I didn't take lightly.

At the time, I had been quietly pursuing membership in a fraternity I'd admired for years. For nearly two years, I had been working toward this goal, facing delays and setbacks outside of my control. This was supposed to be my year to join their line and finally cross into the brotherhood I'd long aspired to be part of. But when I shared the news of the Bears' opportunity with a member of the fraternity, the response I received was anything but supportive.

"You've got too much going on," they told me. "You need to decide: Are you committed to this or not?"

It was a gut punch. I had worked so hard to get to this point with the fraternity, but I also knew deep down that the Bears' offer wasn't something I could pass up. I had to make a decision, and it wasn't an easy one. I had spent years waiting for this moment, proving my worth, hoping I'd finally get my shot. Moving on from this wasn't just about walking away—it felt like walking away from a version of myself I had spent years building.

After a lot of prayer, reflection, and honest conversations with myself, I realized what I needed to do. I couldn't let this opportunity with the Bears slip away—not when it felt like a door God was opening for me. So, I made the tough call to walk away from the fraternity and focus fully on what I believed was my path forward. Shortly after, I called Matt back to officially accept the position, knowing it would require everything I had to make it work. It wasn't a decision I made lightly, but it was one I made with conviction.

Looking back, I see that moment as one of the first times I truly understood what it meant to trust God's plan over my own. The work I would be doing on game days might not have seemed significant to others—setting up displays, coordinating activations, directing the drumline—but I knew the value of every task. This was about more than just the job. It was about staying obedient to the instincts and opportunities God had placed in front of me, even if it meant letting go of something I'd chased for years.

Accepting the position with the Bears was a leap of faith, and one I would never regret.

Monday through Friday, I attended classes, studied, and worked with the Illinois football team during practices. Saturdays were dedicated to game day at Illinois, where I assisted on the sidelines. And then, as soon as the game was over, I packed up my things and drove two-and-a-half hours to Chicago, arriving just in time for the Bears' home game on Sunday. Once the game was over, I'd drive the 135 miles back to Champaign, ready to start the week all over again.

It was exhausting and exhilarating—a whirlwind of opportunity and responsibility that demanded everything I had. But here's the thing: It taught me the value of resilience and sacrifice. Every mile I drove, every hour of sleep I missed, every moment of exhaustion was worth it because I knew that each of these moments was a stepping stone toward my future. The lessons I learned during that season weren't just about football; they were about life. They were about learning to juggle multiple priorities, about knowing when to sacrifice and when to push through exhaustion. I learned that success doesn't come easy—it requires determination, discipline, and above all faith.

There were moments of doubt, nights when I wondered if I could keep up with the demands of both college and my burgeoning career in sports. There were times when the exhaustion felt overwhelming, but every time doubt crept in, I reminded myself of one thing—faith and fear ask you to believe in something that hasn't happened yet. I could either let fear convince me that I wasn't capable of handling it all, or I could lean into faith and trust that all the sacrifices I was making would pay off. So, I leaned into faith. I trusted that even when the path seemed unclear, I was exactly where I was supposed to be. And that's the thing about faith—it doesn't guarantee that the journey will be easy, but it promises that every step forward is worth it.

That year, the Illini football team had a historic season, advancing to the Rose Bowl. I stood on the sidelines, watching the team I had poured so much into reach incredible heights. It was a moment of pride and reflection. From the South Side of Chicago to the sidelines of a team playing in the Rose Bowl—how far I had come. But more important, it was a testament to the power of persistence and faith.

As I reflect on the past, I find myself questioning if the success was purely the result of hard work, or was there something more at play? How much of our success is determined by our efforts, and how much is shaped by the opportunities we're given and the faith we place in ourselves? This season of my life taught me the power of exposure. The media spotlights the athletes and coaches, but rarely do they showcase the individuals working behind the scenes—the ones who make everything run smoothly. In my community, growing up, the focus was always on "going pro" as an athlete but my experiences showed me that there was so much more to the world of sports. I had seen the inner workings of an NFL team, and it opened my eyes to possibilities I hadn't previously considered.

Have you ever wondered how the things you're exposed to shape your expectations? What haven't you been exposed to that might be limiting your vision of what's possible? How are you managing—or mismanaging—the time and opportunities that have been given to you? These are critical questions that can redefine the trajectory of your life.

This idea of exposure and expectations shaping outcomes is something I've reflected on often, especially when I think about a conversation I had with my friend Wes Moore, now the governor of Maryland. Wes once said to me, "Sometimes we are not only products of our environment, but we are products of our expectations."

That statement resonated with me deeply. Two people can grow up in the same environment, but the expectations they set for themselves can drastically alter their paths in life. Wes's words reminded me of how powerful our expectations can be. His book *The Other Wes Moore* perfectly illustrates this idea. It tells the story of two men with the same name and similar early experiences in low-socioeconomic neighborhoods who ended up on vastly different life paths—Wes became a Rhodes Scholar and renowned author, while the other Wes Moore is serving a life sentence in prison.

The contrast in their stories underscores the importance of mentorship, education, and—most important—expectation. What expectations are you setting for yourself? Are they high enough to propel you forward, or are they limiting your potential? Are they aligned with what you truly want, or are they shaped by what others expect of you?

As I stood on the sidelines of the Rose Bowl, reflecting on my journey, I couldn't help but marvel at how far I had come. Each sacrifice, every long drive, and every challenge had shaped me in ways I hadn't fully realized at the time. In that moment, one truth stood out: Those sacrifices weren't just part of the process—they were the process. They were refining me, preparing me for something greater that I couldn't yet see.

The future was as uncertain as ever, but if there's one thing I had learned along the way, it was this: Progress is made in the unknown. Faith doesn't require knowing every step—it demands taking the next one, even when the destination isn't clear. The path before me wasn't about being fearless; it was about moving forward in spite of fear.

As I prepared to leave Illinois behind, the horizon ahead was full of questions. But one thing was certain: Everything I had faced thus far was preparing me for what was coming next. The road would be new, but the foundation of faith that got me here would carry me through. I didn't need to see the whole path. I just needed to keep walking.

The leap ahead wasn't just about where I was going—it was about who I was becoming. This wasn't just a move; it was a test of faith. It was about stepping into a new chapter of my life, a chapter that would demand more faith, more risk, and more of me than ever before. And so, as I looked ahead, I knew this wasn't just the end of a chapter. It was the beginning of a new one.

CHAPTER 2

From Passed Over to Passover

CHICAGO WINTERS HAVE A WAY OF TESTING YOUR RESOLVE. The biting wind, the snow piling up like barriers, and the sub-zero temperatures that seep through every layer of clothing. It's the kind of cold that doesn't just chill your body, it seeps into your bones, making you question not just where you are, but where you're going. Living in Chicago, I had grown all too familiar with that feeling. It wasn't just the brutal winters that wore on me, but the deeper sense that something in my life needed to shift.

The freezing temperatures, the biting wind that cut through layers of clothing, the icy streets that turned a simple walk into a test of endurance—those were more than just weather patterns. They mirrored the restlessness inside me, the feeling that I had hit a ceiling, that I was circling the same realities without moving forward. I wasn't just battling Chicago's cold, I was battling the frustration of knowing I was capable of more, yet unsure of how to step into it. I had done everything "right" up to this point—gone to college, interned with an NFL team—but where was it leading? How many more doors would I knock on before one finally opened? I had spent years enduring that cold, physically and spiritually, and I knew it was time for a change.

But change isn't always easy, is it? How do you take that first step when the future is uncertain? How do you know if you're moving toward the right thing or running from the wrong one? I found myself at a crossroads, one that would determine not just where I lived, but who I was becoming.

I decided to pursue graduate school, but this decision was more than just an academic one—it was about reshaping my life's trajectory. What guides our decisions in these pivotal moments? Is it logic, passion, or perhaps something more intangible? For me, there were three prerequisites: a place with a strong sports administration program that had deep ties to the professional sports industry, a location that was home to multiple professional sports teams or organizations within reasonable proximity, and most important, a climate warmer than Chicago's.

It might sound trivial, but isn't it true that sometimes the smallest details, like the weather, can shape the most significant decisions in our lives? We think we're choosing based on ambition or passion, but sometimes we're simply craving a change of environment, a shift from what we've always known.

In the words of LeBron James, I decided to take my talents to South Beach and enrolled at St. Thomas University in Miami, Florida. Convincing my longtime friend and college roommate—who had been with me through high school and all four years at the University of Illinois—to pursue his postgraduate endeavors in Miami as well was a stroke of luck. He was accepted to the University of Miami School of Law, and we split the housing costs, which eased the transition to our new lives.

How much of our success is shaped by the people we surround ourselves with? Would my journey have been different without the support and companionship of a close friend? These are the kinds of questions we often overlook until hindsight brings them into focus. It's easy to forget how much our choices are intertwined with the people we share them with.

St. Thomas was an intentional choice for me. No, it wasn't a massive sports powerhouse, but it had something many top-ranked programs didn't—direct access to decision-makers in the industry. Many of their adjunct professors weren't just teaching sports business, they were living it. One of my early professors was the Executive Vice President and General Manager of the NBA's Miami Heat. Another instructor was the head of communications and public relations for NASCAR. Where else could I sit in a classroom and learn directly from the people shaping the industry I wanted to break into? It wasn't about prestige—it was about proximity to opportunity.

Can proximity to greatness alone propel us into success, or is there something more that we need to bring to the table?

Moving to Miami was a huge step of faith for me. I didn't know much about the city outside of what I could find on YouTube. Some of my friends and even mentors questioned my decision to pursue a master's degree in sports administration rather than something more traditional like an MBA or law school. But here's a question we all face at some point: Do we follow the well-trodden path, or do we carve out our own, even when the destination is uncertain?

My heart and passion weren't in those traditional fields. One principle I had learned early on in life was this: One of the worst things you can do in life is choose the right thing at the wrong time. The right thing at the wrong time often ends up becoming a curse, not a blessing. I learned this lesson when I continued gymnastics as a kid. I stuck it out, and by the end of the course, I could do the flips I had dreamed of. Timing, as it turned out, wasn't just about starting something—it was about being willing to finish it. If I wanted to pursue law later, I felt that I could, but I wasn't willing to commit to it immediately, especially when I didn't sense God leading me in that direction.

Breaking into the professional sports industry seemed daunting, especially coming from where I did, unless you had the right connections. Ever since my internship with the Chicago Bears, God had pressed upon me to become a student of the industry. I spent countless hours reading books about the business of sports and visiting the websites of professional teams and leagues. I had a unique way of analyzing people's career trajectories: Whenever I read staff profiles or bios on team websites, I started at the bottom, where their bio often detailed their earliest roles. By reading their journey in reverse—bottom to top—I could follow the steps they took to get where they were. This process helped me understand how they built their careers, brick by brick.

But what drives this obsession with understanding the paths of others? Is it the hope that we might find a road map for our own success, or is it the fear of veering off course?

One morning, during my routine of reading bios, I came across someone who had participated in the staff assistantship program with the Miami Dolphins. Upon learning about the program, I looked it up and discovered that the application deadline was just one week away. It felt like a Godsend, and I quickly applied. But isn't it interesting how often we find ourselves relying on fate, on a divine nudge, to justify the paths we choose?

One key strategy I had learned about landing entry-level opportunities in pro sports was the advantage of being enrolled in school and earning college credit while working for the team. Most entry roles weren't full-time positions—they were opportunities that went to students who could lean on their academic standing to gain access, get their foot in the door, and make connections. Being in grad school for sports administration, I knew this was my way in. The full-time roles were as rare as winning the Powerball, but getting into a program like this allowed me to experience the culture, meet key people, and hopefully build a bridge to something more permanent. I waited and waited, following up countless times. I probably called the Dolphins' front desk so often, they could have put me on payroll just for persistence. You would've thought someone there owed me money the way I was calling them.

One morning, before heading to class at St. Thomas, I checked my condo's mailbox, and there it was—a letter from the Miami Dolphins. My heart raced as I quickly rode the elevator back to my unit, my mind swirling with anticipation. But that rush of excitement was short-lived. The letter was short and to the point: I hadn't been accepted into the program. Just like that, everything deflated. I was crushed, disappointed, and felt utterly passed over.

Isn't the sting of rejection a universal feeling? You poured your heart into something, did everything right, only to find yourself on the outside looking in. There's something uniquely painful about chasing after something you believe is meant for you, only to discover that it wasn't. I felt like I had followed all the right steps, played by the rules, and yet still found myself in the wrong place.

> *Isn't the sting of rejection a universal feeling?*

I reread the rejection letter, hoping maybe I had misinterpreted it. Maybe there was still a chance. Maybe a follow-up email could change things. But there it was—clear, final, nonnegotiable.

Had I miscalculated? I had followed every piece of advice, done everything right. So why wasn't it enough? The rejection stung not just because I wanted the job but because I had convinced myself that this was the path—the one God had opened for me. If it wasn't this, then what?

Maybe I needed to let go of control. But what does it mean to let go and let God? Was faith really about surrendering, or was that just what people said when things didn't go their way?

It was in that moment, after reading the rejection letter, that a profound truth hit me: My studious, calculated approach to breaking into the pro-sports world wasn't going to be enough. Sure, I had done the groundwork, but it was going to take more than just my natural abilities. It would require something supernatural—a move of God. But what does that even mean? How do you reconcile the need for hard work and preparation with the belief in something greater, something beyond your control?

As time passed and I continued my studies at St. Thomas, another opportunity opened up. I took on a role as a staff assistant for the St. Thomas University men's basketball team—an experience that would ultimately shape me in ways I hadn't expected. The program wasn't part of the elite NCAA D1, D2, or even D3 leagues. Instead, it was part of the National Association of Intercollegiate Athletics (NAIA) and had a strong tradition of developing student-athletes and instilling values that extended far beyond the game. It wasn't the big leagues, but it was an opportunity to serve and grow.

Of course, I was disappointed. My dream had always been to work at the highest level in sports—the NFL—but here I was, in a smaller, quieter arena. Still, I recognized that St. Thomas had given me something invaluable—a chance to step into sports management in a way that was hands-on, personal, and formative. The job paid decently for a grad student, and I was still working in sports. Isn't it strange how life sometimes gives you exactly what you need, even if it's not what you thought you wanted? I now believe these so-called detours aren't mistakes, but necessary steps in your journey.

That season, working with the men's basketball team became a critical lesson in stewardship. It wasn't about the level I was at, it was about what I did with the opportunity God had given me. Even though it wasn't the glamorous role I had envisioned, I was still building relationships, learning, and most important, championing what was right in front of me. How often are we caught up in something and overlook the value of where we are? What if the present, no matter how humble, is the proving ground for what's coming next?

As I focused on making the most of this season, I learned something else: Stewardship isn't just about managing what you've been given; it's about preparing for what's ahead, even when you can't see it. It's about trusting that every small step you take is leading toward something greater.

In the spring of 2010, about a year had passed since I had taken on the role with the men's basketball team. I decided to visit my parents during Easter weekend, which coincided with the Jewish holiday of Passover. As I returned to Family Christian Center, my family's church, I didn't expect that weekend to mark a pivotal shift in my life.

That Sunday, Pastor Steve Munsey was delivering the message. I wasn't familiar with him, but there was something in his delivery—something in the way he illustrated stories from the Bible—that was different. He had a way of explaining God's ability to perform miracles if we had faith and believed.

While Family Christian Center is nondenominational, Pastor Munsey often emphasized three key seasons on God's calendar: the Passover season (which includes Passover, Unleavened Bread, and First Fruits); the Feast of Weeks—also known as Pentecost (Shavuot in Hebrew); and the Tabernacles season (which includes the Feast of Trumpets, the Day of Atonement, and the Feast of Tabernacles). He taught that these three feast seasons represent divine moments—three sacred links between God and His covenant children—each revealing supernatural truths and blessings, especially through the observance of Passover. These biblical feasts were observances I had previously associated more with the Jewish faith than with Christian practice. But that day, I realized something profound: Faith isn't bound by tradition. Isn't it fascinating how different perspectives can open up new dimensions of understanding? Pastor Munsey taught that these appointed feast days were sacred moments when God invites His people to stand before Him with reverence—and with an offering. Not to earn salvation, but as an act of obedience and alignment with His covenant promises.

What struck me most wasn't just the theological insight—it was the idea that through our obedience on these feast days, God would bless us in the supernatural. The word *supernatural* hit me hard. I was doing everything "right"—studying, networking, applying, calling—but maybe what I needed was something beyond the natural. Something only God could do.

During the offering portion of the service, I felt a tug in my spirit. I reached into my pocket and realized I only had one bill: a $50 bill. It was all I had left, the last bit of cash I had set aside for my visit home. My fear told me to keep it for myself. But faith? Faith was whispering something else entirely. Was this what surrender looked like? Not just believing God could move, but putting something on the line before I saw proof? **That's the nature of faith. It asks you to release what's in your hand so that God can release what's in His.** With a deep breath, I put the bill in the offering bucket, saying silently, "I trust you, God."

The next day, I caught an early morning flight from Chicago back to Miami after the holiday weekend. As the plane ascended into the clouds, I couldn't help but wonder, *Did God even notice what I did yesterday?* My mind was racing. *Will it matter?* Isn't that the internal struggle we often face? The tension between faith and doubt, between the act of trust and the fear that maybe nothing will change.

As the plane began its descent into Miami, I turned my phone back on and immediately saw I had a voicemail. The number wasn't familiar, but something about seeing that missed call made my heart skip a beat. I thought, *Who would have called this early?*

While I navigated through the terminal, I put the phone to my ear and listened to the voicemail. The voice on the other end introduced himself as Jason Jenkins, from the Miami Dolphins. I nearly froze in place. The Miami Dolphins? I hadn't heard that name in months, not since I was passed over for the very program I had poured my hopes into. Jason Jenkins was calling to invite me to interview for the staff assistantship program in media relations. I felt like I had stepped into the supernatural, into the very thing that had been promised. How often do we find ourselves at the intersection of faith and manifestation, only to realize it's all been aligning behind the scenes?

Within days, I went through two interviews and was offered the position. Just like that, I went from being passed over to stepping into the very opportunity I had been praying for. The timing was undeniable. It wasn't just a coincidence—it was a direct response to the faith I had placed in God. I had trusted Him with my finances and my future, and here He was, showing me that He had seen it all.

But what does this teach us about timing? Is there really such a thing as coincidence, or are we part of a larger plan we can't always see? What I realized in that moment is that faith is more than just belief; it's the patience to wait and the courage to act when the moment arrives.

The pastor at my parents' church learned of my story—the miracle that transpired with the Dolphins—and he reached out to me. His message was clear: What had happened was more than just an answered prayer, it was a divine appointment. He connected me with a local church in Miami, Trinity Church Miami, led by pastors Rich Wilkerson Sr. and Dr. Robyn Wilkerson. I didn't know it then, but this church would become a place of refuge, a spiritual home during my time in grad school.

There, my faith deepened in ways I hadn't anticipated. I wasn't just learning about faith; I was learning to walk in it daily. Each sermon, each conversation with people at the church, reinforced something I had begun to internalize: that the faith we're called to is not passive. It's active, alive, and tangible. It's one thing to believe but another to trust in a way that leads to action.

I reflected on the journey that brought me here. It wasn't lost on me that I had prayed so fervently to work with the Dolphins, only to be placed with the men's basketball team at an NAIA school. At the time, it felt like I was off course, that maybe I had misheard what God wanted for me. What I've learned is faith requires trust, even when the path seems unclear. Now I understand that working for the basketball team wasn't a mistake, it was preparation. It was God's way of teaching me stewardship. Sometimes what feels like a detour is actually God setting the stage for something greater. But how often do we dismiss the small steps because they don't look like the big dreams we're holding on to? How often do we fail to see that God is shaping us in the waiting, in the stillness, in the places that feel like they don't matter?

In this season, I learned something that stayed with me: Don't run from what you prayed for, even when God's answer looks different than what you hoped for. God's delays are not denials. That truth reshaped my perspective on disappointment and detours, teaching me that sometimes the answer to our prayers is different because God's vision for us is greater than our own—because sometimes God's plans look different from our own.

As my time with the Miami Dolphins neared its end, I found myself at a pivotal inflection point: What next, God? The assistant-ship had been a blessing, but it wasn't a full-time role with benefits. For many of my elders, especially, landing a job with benefits meant you had "made it." Anything less, no matter how impressive, wasn't recognized as crossing the finish line. And yet, here I was feeling like I was still at the starting gate.

The NFL was also entering a period of uncertainty. The league's collective bargaining agreement (CBA) with the NFL Players Association was set to expire and negotiations were tense. The possibility of an NFL lockout loomed large, and with that uncertainty, teams were freezing hiring and promotions. The grim reality was that I could be at the end of my assistantship, only to find myself back at square one—looking for the next opportunity.

I had been intentional throughout my time with the Dolphins. I knew that networking wasn't just about handing out business cards or trying to make superficial connections. It was about building meaningful relationships. During my time in the industry, I diligently stayed in touch with people who could offer guidance, advice, or opportunities. One such person was Andrew, the man I had shared that last cafeteria meal with during my Chicago Bears internship. Five years had passed since then, and our connection had grown deeper.

Unbeknownst to me at the time, Andrew had been working closely with Lovie Smith, the head coach of the Chicago Bears— the same Lovie Smith who made history as the first-ever African American NFL head coach to advance to the Super Bowl. As Andrew and I caught up on a phone call, I shared with him where I was in my career, the ups and downs of my Dolphins experience, and my search for the next step. I started the interview process for the only job lead I had at the time, which was an entry-level role with the NFL Network.

Toward the end of our call, Andrew dropped an unexpected question: "Lovie is looking for someone to fill a unique role on his staff. Would you be interested? I can recommend you if you'd like."

"What's the role?" I asked, trying to temper my excitement.

"Assistant to the Head Coach."

I almost dropped the phone.

Being the right hand to the head coach of an NFL team—let alone my hometown Chicago Bears—was beyond anything I had imagined. After all, breaking into the pro-sports world is hard enough. Becoming the right hand to a veteran head coach that many in the industry deeply respected felt like a dream.

I immediately sent Andrew my résumé and cover letter, trying not to let my hopes get too high. Even though I had the connection, I knew how competitive the industry was, and I had learned not to count my chickens before they hatched. Weeks went by, and in the meantime, I completed the interview process with the NFL Network. They offered me a full-time position. It wasn't exactly what I had hoped for, but it was still a significant opportunity—with a catch. Due to the NFL lockout and ongoing CBA negotiations, I wouldn't be paid my full salary until the CBA was resolved and ratified. It was a risk, but a full-time job offer nonetheless. Yet something inside me kept holding out for Chicago, for Lovie Smith, for that once-in-a-lifetime opportunity.

I waited. I called Andrew multiple times, leaving messages, hoping for some sign, some clue as to what was happening on the Bears' end. Most of the time, I heard nothing. When Andrew finally did get back to me, he didn't have any updates and advised me to wait it out so as not to pressure Lovie. As the deadline to give the NFL Network my final decision approached, I was torn. Should I settle for the opportunity in front of me, or continue to wait for the one I believed in my heart was meant for me?

On the final day to notify the NFL Network of my decision, I still hadn't heard back from Andrew or the Chicago Bears. The stress, the uncertainty, the silence—it all felt like too much. The same feelings I had experienced when I first applied for the Miami Dolphins role, only to be rejected, resurfaced. I thought about all the steps I had taken—the effort, the relationships, the persistence—and yet, here I was again, seemingly stuck at the precipice of disappointment.

I decided to take a walk, to clear my head and pray. I needed to hear from God. I needed to understand what I was supposed to do. Living in downtown Miami at the time, I walked to Bayfront Park, the closest body of water I could find. I walked slowly toward the edge, and as soon as I reached it, the emotions I had been holding in came pouring out. I began to cry—uncontrollably. I didn't care who was around, who saw me, or what they thought. I just let it all out. As I stood there, staring out at the water, I began crying out to God, asking, "Why would you bring me this far, only to leave me like this? What was the purpose of all the sacrifice, all the prayers, if this is how it ends?"

And that's when it happened.

A prompting in my spirit—an inner voice—rose up within me. It felt like God was speaking directly to me, not in an audible voice, but in a way that I felt deep in my soul.

"Michael," the voice said, "look at this water in front of you. In order to get to what you know is possible, you're going to have to walk on this water."

I paused, confused by what I had just heard. Walk on water? Wasn't faith supposed to feel easier than this?

What if I took that step and nothing happened? What if I stepped out and sank?

The voice returned, this time even clearer: "In order to get to what you know is possible, you're going to have to walk on what everyone else in the world often deems impossible—your faith."

And then, something shifted.

In that moment, I realized God was trying to remind me that I had been walking on water this whole time. Every risk, every moment I had trusted without seeing the outcome, had led me here. I had already proven I could take steps of faith. And now, it was time for the next one.

Immediately, I felt a sense of peace wash over me. It was as if the burden I had been carrying was lifted, and I knew—deep down— that everything would be okay.

I whispered to myself, "I still trust you, God," and began walking back to my apartment, my heart lighter than it had been in weeks.

As I stepped through my front door, my phone started to ring. I glanced at the screen and saw a 312-area code—Chicago. My heart skipped a beat.

I answered, and the first words I heard were, "Hello, Michael, it's Coach Lovie Smith with the Bears."

====

In that instant, time seemed to stand still. On the very day I had to make a decision about the role with the NFL Network—the role I wasn't entirely sure was for me—I received the job offer I had been praying for. Weeks later, at the age of twenty-four, I became the Assistant to the Head Coach for the Chicago Bears.

It felt surreal. To go from standing on the edge of despair, questioning everything, to receiving a call that would change the course of my life—it was a reminder that God's timing is always perfect. Just when we think we're at our breaking point, when we're ready to give up, that's when the breakthrough happens. That's when we realize that faith isn't just about waiting—it's about trusting the process, even when it doesn't make sense.

And that's what I learned in this moment: What God has for you is for you. No one can take it away. It's already written. It's just a matter of aligning your faith with His timing.

This experience taught me that having faith in God also means having faith in His timing. Timing is one of the hardest things to balance in life—waiting for the right door to open without forcing it, believing that the right opportunity will come at the right moment. To the person reading this, wondering if your faith can open that door you're currently hoping for—yes, it can, and it will. You may be one of the most influential and wealthy people in your family, or you might be wondering where your next meal is coming from. Regardless of who you are or where you are, the principle remains the same. Keep believing, keep trusting, and keep moving forward. You are one step of faith away from a new season in your life.

Becoming the right hand to an NFL head coach came with more than just prestige—it came with unique access, influence, and responsibility. Serving as the liaison between Coach Lovie Smith and a host of powerful figures inside and outside the world of sports became the norm for me. I soon realized that this role wasn't just about handling day-to-day logistics or managing schedules. It was about learning leadership on an intimate, firsthand level. I had a front-row seat to see how decisions were made, how crises were handled, and how influence was wielded.

What intrigued me most was how my interactions with NFL headquarters staff always seemed to carry a different weight. They had a level of insight that extended beyond just one team—they had a comprehensive view of the entire NFL landscape. They weren't focused on one franchise's success; they were managing the business of football across thirty-two teams, influencing league-wide strategies and policies. Why is it that some people can zoom out and see the entire playing field, while others are only focused on their small part of the game?

I began to ask myself a fundamental question: What does it take to elevate your perspective? To not only see the big picture but to become a part of shaping it?

One person who inspired this shift in my thinking was Pete Abi-tante, the Special Assistant to the Commissioner. Pete had worked with the NFL Commissioner since the early 1980s, serving for decades in a key role shaping policies at the league level. I first met Pete during a Bears training camp when the NFL Commissioner announced that he would embark on a training camp tour of select NFL team locations, and Chicago was one of the cities on his stop. Accompanying him on this tour was none other than the late, great Hall of Fame coach John Madden. The energy, excitement, and anticipation surrounding the visit from the league's most powerful individual and the legendary Coach Madden were palpable throughout the facility.

It was common for VIP visitors to coordinate directly with me to arrange time with Coach Smith, but this visit stood out. I had the chance to engage with Pete, share my journey with him, and learn about his experiences at the league office. He listened attentively, and before the conversation ended, he gave me his contact information and told me to reach out if I ever needed advice or support. That brief interaction planted a seed in my mind. Here was someone who wasn't just involved with one team—he was shaping policies that impacted the entire league. That level of leadership and influence was something that spoke to me. I could feel the wheels turning in my head. Why settle for just being the assistant to a leader when I could become a leader myself? Why limit my vision to one team when there was an opportunity to shape the future of the entire NFL?

As I left that conversation with Pete, I felt a surge of excitement mixed with reflection. I couldn't help but think back to my childhood, to that young boy on the South Side of Chicago who rode his bike up and down the same sidewalk, not knowing what it must feel like to go beyond the barriers of an environment I knew, felt safe in, and was accustomed to. There had to be something more, something bigger inside of me than what was around me. That same feeling stirred within me now—an inner calling, reminding me that there was a greater horizon waiting for me to explore.

But here's the thing: Ambition without direction can lead you astray. How do you channel that drive to ensure it doesn't just become a selfish pursuit of power? How do you ensure that your desire to lead is about serving a higher purpose, about making a difference that transcends your own personal success?

As I grew closer to this inner calling, I realized that my vision was expanding. There was a higher purpose guiding me beyond simply being excellent at my current role. It was about using the experience I gained to influence the future in a meaningful way, and that realization would soon lead me to a crossroads—the decision to transition from working for a single NFL team to stepping onto a much larger platform at NFL headquarters.

In 2014, an opportunity emerged at NFL headquarters that marked a significant step forward in the next phase of my journey. I saw it as a great chance to learn about the business of the NFL from a macro perspective, within a department where I could continue to grow. It also seemed like the perfect moment for me to add value. Given my experience working at the NFL team level, I knew I could offer insights and institutional knowledge on the inner workings of a team—insights that would prove beneficial to the Management Council, which many at the team level often felt was too disconnected or removed from the day-to-day operations of teams. Normally, the career trajectory for individuals at the league office involved eventually moving on to work for an individual NFL team. For me, it was the opposite. My interest lay in learning the business as a whole and contributing to the overall impact across all thirty-two NFL teams. I was ready to make the transition from the team level to NFL headquarters.

The role was in the Management Council, the division responsible for representing the billionaire owners and ownership groups
of all NFL teams on matters related to the CBA. The division
required sharp intellect; the ability to navigate complex dynamics between labor, ownership, and league administration; and—
depending on your portfolio of work—some level of legal acumen.
This was a highly respected division within the NFL, handling sen-
sitive business negotiations that impacted the entire league and
worked in service to all NFL teams.

I had heard that the vast majority of people in the Management Council had graduated from Ivy League institutions or were
esteemed attorneys from some of the largest and most influential
law firms in the world. Stepping into this space, I couldn't help
but wonder: Was I truly prepared to work with individuals who
seemed so far removed from the world I came from? Was I ready
to keep up with their backgrounds and credentials?

Despite my apprehension, I felt that everything I had been
through had prepared me for this moment. Every challenge, every
lesson was guiding me toward this new chapter. I couldn't allow
doubt or fear to overshadow the faith that had brought me this
far. I had been walking on water before, and this was no different. Through persistence, preparation, and the relationships I had
built—particularly with Pete Abitante and another NFL league
office staffer who had previously worked with me during my time
in Chicago with the Bears—I was granted an opportunity to interview for the role. By the grace of God, I nailed it and was offered
the position.

Accepting the role meant more than just advancing my career;
it also meant leaving Chicago and moving to New York City—a
step that felt both exciting and daunting. Moving to NYC came
with its own unique challenges. The cost of living was significantly
higher, a reality I often joked about with friends: "In New York,

you pay twice as much for half the space." But beyond the financial adjustment, there was the weight of leaving behind the comfort of familiarity and stepping into the unknown.

Mentors in my circle helped ease my anxieties. They reminded me that New York City wasn't just a destination; it was a hub of opportunity—a place where leaders across professional sports and countless other industries converged. They encouraged me to view the move not as an obstacle but as a gateway to building relationships and expanding my network in ways that would prove invaluable down the road. Their advice stayed with me, anchoring my faith that this move was part of a much larger plan.

However, not everyone in my circle agreed. Some urged me to stay in Chicago, pointing to the Bears' recent progress under then new head coach, Marc Trestman, whom I had admired and grown close with. With the 2013 Bears offense finishing as the second-best scoring offense in the league, they believed I could be leaving just as the team was on the brink of a successful stretch—possibly even playoff appearances or a Super Bowl run. They cautioned me against walking away too soon, fearing I might regret it.

It was a difficult tension to sit with, but ultimately, I knew whose voice I needed to prioritize. God had been preparing me for this moment, and I could feel His prompting to step into something new. Sometimes even the well-intentioned advice of others isn't in alignment with what God is calling you to do. I've learned that trusting God's plan often means walking away from what's comfortable or promising in the short term to embrace a future that only He can see. Obedience to God's voice isn't always easy, but it's always necessary.

I was stepping into NFL headquarters, into a division where I could contribute to the future of the league on a grand scale, and this achievement was deeply humbling. I knew that many people from my background didn't have the opportunity to make it this far. I also knew this moment was bigger than me. It was about representation, about breaking barriers, and about creating a path for others who would follow.

And yet, my excitement quickly turned into anxiety. The weight of being the only Black staff member on the Labor Operations team hit me. Most of my colleagues had prestigious degrees and qualifications that seemed, on the surface, far more impressive than my own. Could I measure up? Could I keep up with them?

I made a decision: I would remain humble, put my head down, and learn from everyone around me. I would absorb whatever lessons this new environment had to offer, and most important, I would trust that God had brought me here for a reason. There's a quote that I have heard throughout my life: "Never stop learning because life never stops teaching." That became my mantra during those early days. The Management Council, led by Jeff Pash, the NFL's Executive Vice President and General Counsel, and Peter Ruocco, the Senior Vice President of Labor Relations, was incredibly welcoming. They poured into me, teaching me not just the business of football but how to navigate the intricacies of labor relations at the highest levels. My other colleagues in the Labor Operations group were also instrumental in helping me learn the ropes. I had the privilege of working with a team that was willing to invest in me and help expand my portfolio beyond my original role.

It was through Jeff, Peter, and several of my colleagues that I was nominated to take on a leadership role within the NFL's diversity and inclusion efforts across the thirty-two NFL teams. This marked a pivotal shift—not just in my career but in my mission to contribute meaningfully to the league's broader impact. As I continued growing at NFL headquarters and delving deeper into the business, I was also drawn to the league's diversity and inclusion efforts. Jeff and my colleagues in the Labor Operations group had recognized my passion and leadership potential in this area, and they supported me in taking on more responsibilities related to DEI initiatives.

One of my first significant roles in this space was helping to lead the NFL Diversity Council, as well as managing the NFL Bill Walsh Diversity Coaching Fellowship program. The fellowship was created to diversify the coaching talent pipeline and give talented minority coaches opportunities to gain experience with NFL teams during training camps, offseason workout programs, and minicamps. This program was designed as a vocational tool to increase the number of full-time NFL minority coaches. All NFL teams participated, which meant the program had the potential to make a real difference in the representation of minority coaches in the NFL.

I had noticed during my time at the individual NFL team level that the selection process for participants or prospective coaches in the fellowship program could improve and grow more equitable in its approach. For example, assistant coaches would often approach me since I was the primary administrator of the team's program, asking if a friend, neighbor, or someone they knew could be brought into the program—sometimes with little regard for the individual's qualifications or true interest in coaching. The program, intended to level the playing field, could have easily become yet another gatekeeping mechanism, a way to reinforce existing connections rather than opening doors for deserving but often overlooked talent.

I wanted to change that.

Though I was now working at NFL headquarters, I often reflected on the success stories I'd witnessed in the past. One story in particular stayed with me, a clear example of how attention and intention within the Bill Walsh Diversity Coaching Fellowship could yield amazing outcomes and truly change lives. It was a success story that underscored my belief in the power of the program and in the importance of casting a wider net to find those who might otherwise be overlooked.

In 2013, while working with the Chicago Bears, I had aligned with the Head Coach to establish a more structured and intentional selection committee for the Bill Walsh Diversity Coaching Fellowship. This committee, made up of assistant coaches and me, reviewed hundreds of applications and conducted interviews with candidates who had historically been passed over. One such candidate was Marquice Williams, an African American coach from the University of South Dakota. He had applied to the fellowship multiple times over the course of four years but had never been selected.

We interviewed him over the phone—this was before virtual meetings became the norm—and Marquice's insight and enthusiasm stood out immediately. He was selected to participate with the Bears, and during his time with the team, he not only made meaningful connections but also left a lasting impression on the coaching staff. Marquice's journey was a powerful reminder of why the program existed in the first place: to give a fair shot to talented coaches like him, whose potential might otherwise go unnoticed due to a system that often relied too heavily on personal connections.

Ten years later, Marquice would go on to become the Special Teams Coordinator for the Atlanta Falcons. His success story demonstrated the life-changing power of an equitable approach to opportunity and the impact that intentional leadership can have on the trajectory of a person's career. For me, this experience reinforced the importance of DEI initiatives, not just as a professional responsibility but as part of my personal mission. DEI isn't just about individual success stories; it's about changing the system. Giving attention and intention to inequitable structures that exist in our organizations has the potential to change not only a person's life but also their family and their community. It's about creating ripples that extend far beyond the immediate impact.

The NFL's Bill Walsh Diversity Coaching Fellowship was just one part of a broader commitment I had begun to feel deeply connected to—a commitment to making sure the spaces I entered were inclusive and equitable. As I grew in my role at NFL headquarters, it became clearer that my purpose wasn't just to advance within the league but to contribute to something much larger. Each new experience, whether in diversity initiatives or the lessons I learned from my colleagues and mentors, wasn't simply about career development; it was about laying the groundwork for how I could help transform the spaces around me. It wasn't just about finding my place in the NFL; it was about making space for others, challenging norms, and pushing for equity at every level.

What do we do when faced with the impossible? How do we navigate the tension between our ideals and the realities we encounter? These are the moments that test not just our faith but our purpose. The initiatives I led, the people I met, and the lessons I learned were shaping not only my career but my understanding of what truly mattered to me.

I had been drawn to diversity and inclusion work, sensing that my contribution to the league had to go beyond wins, losses, or even labor relations. I felt a deeper call to help create spaces where everyone could thrive, regardless of their background or circumstances. That calling would soon come into sharper focus. Little did I know that the next chapter of my journey would challenge me—and the league—in ways I couldn't have anticipated.

As I continued to reflect on where my career was heading, the NFL was about to face a moment that would not only shake the league but spark a national conversation. The tension between ideals and reality was about to be felt in an entirely different way.

CHAPTER 3

Taking a Stand

The Kaepernick Effect

ONE RAINY MORNING IN SEPTEMBER 2016, I GLANCED AT MY phone, half-distracted as I grabbed my bag for work. But then I saw the name on my screen—a seismic shift happened. Before leaving my apartment for the office, my phone buzzed with a series of alerts. The name that kept flashing on the screen was familiar: Colin Kaepernick.

The headlines painted a picture that grabbed my attention:

"Colin Kaepernick's National Anthem Protest Draws
    Strong Reactions" (CNN)
"Patriotism or Disrespect?" (Fox News)
"Colin Kaepernick Sits During the National Anthem"
    (*Sports Illustrated*)
"Kaepernick's Protest Divides NFL Fans" (ESPN)

It was that last headline that stuck with me. Divides NFL fans? The NFL, in my mind, had always been seen as a unifying force—a place where people, despite their differences, could come together to cheer on their favorite teams. The notion that the league could suddenly be a source of division felt foreign. After all, wasn't the beauty of sports in its power to transcend the very divisions that often plague society?

As I read further into the details of Kaepernick's protest—his decision to sit during the national anthem as a stand against police brutality and racial injustice—I assumed this would be short-lived. The NFL, I thought, would surely address this with a statement in solidarity with his concerns. After all, incidents of racial injustice had been plastered across headlines for years, and with the vast majority of players in the NFL being Black, I expected a straightforward stance from the league. But I was wrong.

This wasn't just about Kaepernick. His silent protest was a response to names etched into the national consciousness—Trayvon Martin, Michael Brown, Eric Garner, Tamir Rice, Sandra Bland, Freddie Gray, Alton Sterling, Philando Castile. These weren't just headlines; they were lives cut short in ways that felt unjust, sparking grief, outrage, and calls for change. Each name carried a story, a family, a community, and a reminder of the fragile line between life and tragedy for so many Black Americans. These weren't isolated events—they were part of a pattern, a stark reflection of systemic inequality that had become impossible to ignore.

For many in the league—players, staff, and fans alike—this wasn't abstract. These were the stories they lived, the conversations they had with their families, the fears they carried when stepping outside their doors. I thought about the quiet, knowing nods exchanged between Black colleagues in the hallways, the side conversations that never made it into official meetings. We all had our own stories—run-ins with police that could've gone another way, relatives whose names could have easily been on that "list." Kaepernick's protest wasn't just a moment of defiance; it was a mirror held up to a nation that often struggled to reconcile its ideals with its realities.

And yet, amid the tension, there was an eerie silence—a pause that spoke louder than words. The NFL, an institution revered for its ability to unite people across divides, suddenly found itself at the center of one. The very idea of division within the league felt foreign. Football was supposed to be the great equalizer—the place where race, politics, and social issues were left at the gate—but here we were, and the divisions were undeniable.

When I arrived at work that day, the energy felt different. There was an undercurrent of tension in every conversation about Kaepernick's protest. This controversy wasn't just making waves in the media—it was stirring something deeper within the NFL itself. Kaepernick's silent act had sparked a loud and uncomfortable question—one that couldn't be ignored: What do we truly stand for? When the world you thought you knew begins shifting beneath your feet, how do you find steady ground? For the league, finding that footing required more than just responding to the public. It demanded a deeper reckoning within its own walls—a recognition that systemic change starts from within.

> *When the world you thought you knew begins shifting beneath your feet, how do you find steady ground?*

The Formation of the NFL's Black Engagement Network

As the league wrestled with the public's reaction to Kaepernick, another shift was happening internally—one that would prove equally significant. The NFL's Black Engagement Network (BEN) was formed in response to a growing need to not only attract and retain Black talent but to create a space where Black employees could thrive. The mission was bold: to foster professional development, mentorship, and career management, while promoting an understanding of Black employees and their contributions across the organization. Could creating an affinity group truly address the systemic issues in society, or was it simply a step toward a deeper commitment to change?

One of BEN's standout initiatives during this charged period was a series of fireside chats and listening sessions. These sessions brought NFL staff, particularly BEN members, face-to-face with the most senior leaders and influencers at the league, providing an opportunity to engage with them on both a professional and personal level. One of those initial sessions featured none other than Commissioner Roger Goodell, a man whose influence extended far beyond the NFL, shaping the broader landscape of American sports. But what does it mean to wield that kind of influence? How does one leader's vision shape the future of an entire league?

The fireside chat with Roger Goodell wasn't just another meeting—it was an opportunity for BEN members to ask meaningful, pressing questions. The conversation started in familiar territory—focused on career development, leadership principles, and strategies for growth within the league. But as the session wore on, a topic emerged that couldn't be avoided: Colin Kaepernick's protest.

In private discussions, BEN members had already expressed a desire to know where the league stood—not just in terms of policy but in its core values. How would the NFL respond to the societal issues that Kaepernick had brought to light? Would the league recognize and address the same injustices that many of its players and employees faced outside the stadiums? It was a delicate and important topic, one that couldn't be sidestepped.

Goodell listened intently, pausing before he responded. When he did, his message centered on a theme he would revisit in the years to come—"Moving from protest to progress." He acknowledged the weight of the protests but emphasized the need to focus on making tangible progress on the issues rather than the protest itself. While his response was measured, I could sense that it left lingering questions unspoken by some of the BEN members in the room.

As the session came to an end, I couldn't help but feel that something more was needed—something beyond corporate responses and public statements. The room didn't quite settle. You could feel it in the way some people nodded along, but their expressions told another story—one of quiet calculation, of wondering what would actually change in the world. It was the kind of moment where the words spoken were less important than the ones left unsaid. It felt like a crossroads moment for the league and for those of us inside it. How would we ensure that Kaepernick's call for justice wouldn't just fade into the noise of the news cycle?

Personal Reflections and Historical Parallels

Reflecting on Goodell's words and the league's response to Kaepernick, I couldn't shake the feeling that more could be done—not just as NFL employees but as a society. There was a unique power in partnering with athletes to push for social change, especially in Black and Brown communities. History has shown that athletes, with their visibility and platforms, have often been the ones to draw attention to societal injustices. But why do we so often see this pattern—where those in the sports world, who are expected to entertain, end up becoming voices for change? Is it because their stage is so public or because their courage speaks to something universal in us all?

I thought back to other pivotal moments in sports history. In 1968, Olympians Tommie Smith and John Carlos raised their fists in a Black Power salute during the medal ceremony, an iconic image that came with heavy consequences—expulsion from the Games and enduring backlash. In 2014, LeBron James and Derrick Rose wore I CAN'T BREATHE shirts during warm-ups to protest the death of Eric Garner, who had died after being placed in a chokehold by police. These were athletes using their platforms to draw attention to systemic issues, risking their careers and public standing to make a statement.

As Kaepernick's story unfolded, I found myself grappling with a question: What is it about sports and protest that makes them so potent, so intertwined? Athletes, often seen as figures of physical prowess, become powerful symbols of resistance when they use their visibility to stand against the status quo. But is it only the weight of their fame, or is there a deeper, more profound connection between sport and social justice?

The Kaepernick Effect: A Personal Turning Point

As the 2016 NFL season progressed, the ripple effects of Kaepernick's protest continued to grow. While Kaepernick's stance sparked a national debate, I couldn't help but reflect on how it impacted the NFL internally. There was a certain unease within the league, particularly among employees like me who felt a deep connection to the issues Kaepernick was highlighting.

At the time, my role was focused on labor relations—hours spent reviewing player contracts, advising team personnel on CBA-related matters, and immersing myself in the business side of the league. I had volunteered my time to lead DEI-related initiatives, but that was never my full-time responsibility. The work

I was doing was important, but I started to question whether it was enough. Was I really contributing to the kind of change that mattered most to me?

As Kaepernick remained unsigned by the end of the 2016 season, it became clear that his protest was not just about taking a knee—it was about the price of speaking out. Despite leading the 49ers to a Super Bowl appearance just a few years earlier, Kaepernick was now without a team. The media framed his lack of a contract as a business decision, but to those paying closer attention, it felt like something more. It raised an uncomfortable question: What is the true cost of standing up for what you believe in?

I had seen this pattern before. Black athletes, and Black people in general, who spoke out against injustice were often ostracized, told that they should be grateful for the opportunities they had. Kaepernick's story felt like a modern version of a very old narrative—one that I had observed in my own life and career, and one that countless others had experienced. The unspoken message was clear: You can succeed in this world, but only if you don't rock the boat.

The more I thought about it, the more I questioned my own path. Was I being called to stay in labor relations, or was there something else I should be doing? Something more aligned with my growing interest in diversity, equity, and inclusion? How do you know when it's time to shift directions, especially when that shift requires leaving behind something you've worked so hard to build?

The week that Kaepernick's protest gained significant media attention coincided with Labor Day, a holiday rooted in the history of American workers fighting for fair treatment. It was a poignant parallel for me, especially given my role in labor relations. Labor Day, ironically, was one of the busiest times of the year for our team in the NFL Management Council. The NFL preseason had just ended, a period when teams could expand their rosters to evaluate players beyond the regular season limit. With the regular season approaching, teams had to make final decisions on their rosters, leading to a flurry of player transactions, contracts, and last-minute approvals. Our department was responsible for auditing and approving all of these moves.

Isn't it ironic that a day meant to honor labor often demands the most laborious efforts? The holiday itself, meant to recognize workers' rights, contrasted sharply with the heavy workload we faced that week. And as I navigated the complex realities of my job, the societal struggle Kaepernick was highlighting grew increasingly clear.

Labor Day and the Pullman Strike: A Historical Parallel

Labor Day has its roots in the labor movement, a time when workers fought for their rights and demanded recognition for their contributions to society. The first Labor Day was celebrated on September 5, 1882, in New York City, and it became a federal holiday in 1894, following the Pullman Strike. The irony wasn't lost on me—the Pullman Strike, which took place in my hometown of Chicago, was a defining moment in American labor history, and here I was, more than a century later, navigating labor relations in a league at the center of a national conversation on justice and inequality.

The Pullman Strike was more than a protest; it was an act of survival. The Pullman Company didn't just employ its workers—it controlled much of their daily lives. The company owned a substantial portion of the town where many of its workers lived, including their homes, shops they frequented, schools, and even churches. Though workers were not required to live in the company town, many chose to because of the quality of housing and amenities available—options that were superior to those elsewhere at the time. However, this arrangement created a dynamic where workers often felt beholden to the company for both their livelihoods and their living conditions. It was a carefully constructed company town.

When the Pullman Company slashed wages during an economic downturn in 1894, it did not reduce rents or living expenses in its company-owned properties. Workers faced the cruel paradox of earning less while still paying the same—or even more—for housing and necessities, often handing back much of their diminished earnings to the very employer who had cut their pay. This disparity sparked an eventual nationwide strike that brought the railroad industry to a standstill and highlighted the power imbalance between labor and management.

The parallels to Colin Kaepernick's protest and the broader dynamics within the NFL were striking. Like the Pullman workers, NFL players operate within a system of concentrated power. NFL owners, who oversee billion-dollar franchises, play a significant role in shaping the terms of players' careers and working conditions. The collective bargaining agreement between the league and the players underscores a collaborative effort, but it also highlights the inherent tension that can arise when one group holds more influence over the structure of the system.

Doesn't it resonate how power dynamics—whether in business or society—often shape the experiences of those navigating them?

For me, the parallels were clear. Kaepernick, like the Pullman workers, was challenging a system that had long resisted calls for change, often ignoring the voices of those most affected by injustice. While his protest was aimed at societal inequalities, the NFL became an unintended focal point, as his platform within the league disrupted its business-as-usual rhythm. This act illuminated the intricate power dynamics—both visible and unseen—within the league and society at large. Much like the Pullman Strike, Kaepernick's protest was met with fierce opposition from those who viewed it as a challenge to the established order. How often do we see history echoing itself, with the same struggles for equity and justice recurring across eras and industries? What does it say about our society when calls for justice are met with resistance, when those who speak out are punished instead of heard? History reminds us that progress often arises from moments of discomfort, when those who dare to disrupt the norm refuse to be silenced.

The Foundations of Protest: Obama's Remarks

On September 5, 2016, President Barack Obama addressed the growing controversy surrounding Colin Kaepernick's decision to kneel during the national anthem. Speaking at a news conference at the conclusion of the G20 summit in China, Obama remarked, "He's exercising his constitutional right to make a statement. I think there's a long history of sports figures doing so." He went on to say, "As a general matter, when it comes to the flag and the national anthem, and the meaning that that holds for our men and women in uniform and those who fought for us, that is a tough thing for them to get past to then hear what his deeper concerns are. But I don't doubt his sincerity, based on what I've heard. I think he cares about some real, legitimate issues that have to be talked about. And if nothing else, what he's done is he's generated more conversation around some topics that need to be talked about."

This day of Obama's remarks was no ordinary one. More coincidence than providence, it landed on the anniversary of America's very first Labor Day in 1882. The irony was palpable: On the very same date that America first formally recognized the labor movement's fight for rights and justice, the president was now defending an athlete's right to protest systemic injustice.

As the nation's first Black president in his final year in office, Obama's defense carried profound weight. He emphasized that Kaepernick was exercising his constitutional right to protest, drawing a powerful parallel between Kaepernick's actions and the broader American ideal of freedom of expression. It is fascinating how the principles of freedom and justice, which are so often invoked as core American values, can be both defended and attacked depending on who is exercising them.

Obama's words were a reminder of the ongoing journey toward equality and freedom—a journey that continues to evolve across generations and contexts. And yet, while his defense carried hope and clarity, the nation remained deeply divided over what Kaepernick's protest represented.

The Evolution of Kaepernick's Protest

As the 2016 NFL season progressed, Kaepernick's protest ignited a firestorm, drawing both support and condemnation. What started as one man's stand against racial injustice had now become the focal point of a national debate. The stark divisions became more apparent as political leaders, media personalities, and fans weighed in on the controversy.

Kaepernick's decision to kneel during the national anthem was not a rash or impulsive act—it was a thoughtful protest against systemic racism and police brutality. Initially, Kaepernick had chosen to sit during the anthem, but after consulting with former NFL player and ex-Green Beret Nate Boyer, he opted to kneel instead. Boyer had suggested kneeling as a sign of respect, even while making a powerful statement. By choosing to kneel, Kaepernick sought to exercise his constitutional right to protest, drawing attention to the critical issues affecting the Black community, while still showing reverence for the flag.

Who gets to define what patriotism looks like, and why is it that some voices are silenced in the name of national pride?

For many, Kaepernick's actions were seen as a betrayal of the flag and the nation's ideals. For others, his protest was a courageous stand for the very values America was built upon—justice, equality, and freedom of expression. The backlash was swift, and the narrative around Kaepernick became less about the issue of police brutality and more about whether or not he was "disrespecting" the country. It is ironic that a nation built on the right to protest finds itself so divided when that right is exercised. Who gets to define what patriotism looks like, and why is it that some voices are silenced in the name of national pride?

Trump's Remarks: A Flashpoint in the Debate

By the following year, the debate over Kaepernick's protest reached a boiling point. On September 22, 2017, then-President Donald Trump reignited the controversy during a rally in Huntsville, Alabama. Speaking to a crowd, Trump declared, "Wouldn't you love to see one of these NFL owners, when somebody disrespects our flag, to say, 'Get that son of a bitch off the field right now, out, he's fired.'"

Trump's remarks sparked outrage and applause in equal measure, polarizing the nation even further. Within days, NFL teams, players, and owners began to respond. Some kneeled during the anthem in solidarity. Others locked arms to show unity. And still others stood, choosing to honor the flag while silently supporting their colleagues' rights to protest. The nation watched as these symbolic gestures played out on the field, but the underlying issues—racial injustice, police brutality, and systemic inequality—remained.

The NFL, often celebrated as a unifier, now found itself as a microcosm of the nation's fractures. Inside league headquarters, the conversations about Kaepernick's protest had shifted from whispers to weighted discussions, echoing the tension felt across the country. The league wasn't just grappling with public perception; it was wrestling with its identity, its purpose, and its future. How could an institution built on teamwork and unity navigate a moment so deeply rooted in division?

Yet what struck me most wasn't just the tension—it was the silence. For all the heated debates outside the league, inside those walls, there was a collective pause, a hesitation to act, to speak, to take a stand. Football, long viewed as an escape from society's challenges, was now a stage for one of its most pressing debates. And as the world watched, waiting for the NFL to choose a side, the league stood in the eye of a cultural storm.

———

Personal Reflections and Professional Challenges

As I observed the reactions from inside and outside the league, it became clear that this wasn't just a conversation about football—it was a conversation about the soul of our country. And in the middle of it all, I found myself reflecting on my role within the NFL. My work in labor relations, while important and deeply connected to the business of the league, felt somewhat disconnected from the broader social issues that were emerging. It wasn't just Kaepernick's protest—it was a combination of events, conversations, and a shifting cultural landscape that made me consider whether I should be more actively involved in the work that spoke to the larger societal issues at hand.

Kaepernick's protest, Obama's remarks, and the national discourse forced me to reconsider whether I was using my platform to its full potential. I valued my role in labor relations and the influence it gave me across the league. I could feel a growing internal pull, a sense that my contribution could and perhaps should extend beyond the business of the league. It wasn't about walking away from what I had worked hard to build, it was about recognizing the moment I was in and leaning into what I felt truly mattered.

The weight of these societal concerns became harder to ignore. Black athletes like Kaepernick were risking everything to stand up for their communities, and the issues they were raising were not foreign to me or to those I knew. In fact, these issues had long been part of my own experience and those of people in my world. Yet here I was, working in an environment where these concerns, while discussed, didn't seem to be fully addressed. Was I doing enough? Was there more I could contribute to the push for equity and justice within this powerful institution?

The Pivotal Moment: A Shift in Purpose

It was a BEN fireside chat with Commissioner Goodell that helped bring these questions I had into sharper focus. While the conversation centered on moving from "protest to progress," it left me thinking more deeply about the role I was playing within the NFL and whether I could be doing more. It wasn't just about climbing the corporate ladder anymore; it was about aligning my work with a higher purpose.

The work that mattered most to me was ensuring that under-represented people and communities felt seen, heard, and valued, particularly in the causes they were fighting for. I realized that driving change meant not only addressing the inequities that existed within the league but also advocating for those who often went unnoticed in the broader societal landscape. The more I reflected on it, the clearer it became that I needed to lean more fully into this work, especially as the world around me was becoming increasingly vocal about these issues.

Moving from Protest to Progress

Years later, in 2020, after the murder of George Floyd, Roger Goodell's stance evolved significantly. He appeared on Emmanuel Acho's podcast, *Uncomfortable Conversations with a Black Man*, where he acknowledged the league's past mistakes and expressed regret for not listening to players sooner. Goodell's apology, released on social media, marked a significant shift in how the league was addressing racial injustice. He admitted that the NFL had been wrong for not listening to players like Kaepernick earlier and openly encouraged peaceful protests, even inviting Kaepernick to return to the league in any capacity, whether on or off the field.

This change in Goodell's perspective, although it came years later, underscored something I had started to realize back then—people and institutions can evolve. It takes time, sometimes far longer than we hope, but transformation is possible. This foreshadowed the shifts that were coming, not just for Goodell and the NFL, but for me as well. As I reflected on my journey, I saw that the work I wanted to dedicate myself to—centered on driving culture through diversity, equity, and inclusion—wasn't just about a career change. It was about making a meaningful impact. Kaepernick's protest sparked a movement that reverberated far beyond the NFL, and it reminded me of the power of individual actions to create collective change. The path from protest to progress isn't linear because it requires persistence, reflection, and the courage to act.

As I looked at the ripple effects of Kaepernick's actions—how one man's decision to kneel stirred conversations across the nation—I realized this moment was a turning point for many of us, including myself. His stand against injustice wasn't just a protest; it was a challenge. A challenge to all of us to examine our roles within the systems we were a part of and to ask ourselves: Were we making the kind of impact we were called to make? Or were we just maintaining the status quo?

I had been reflecting for some time on my own journey, wondering if I was living out the purpose I felt called to. I knew my role within the NFL mattered, but was it enough? The more I thought about it, the more I understood that the path forward for me would require more than just staying the course. It would require stepping into something bigger, more meaningful—a shift from the comfort of what I knew into the unknown of what could be.

I hadn't anticipated where this internal tug would lead, but sometimes the next chapter in our lives isn't one we write ourselves. It's one that reveals itself, slowly at first, then all at once. What I didn't know was how soon that change would come, or in what form. And as I stood at this crossroads, I knew that change was coming. Not just for the league, not just for society—but for me, too.

CHAPTER 4

Answering the Call,
Campaign Catalyst

HOW DID I GET HERE? IT'S A QUESTION THAT SNEAKS UP ON us in the most unexpected moments, usually when life throws us at a crossroads we never saw coming. The ground beneath us feels like it's shifting, and we're left wondering how to reconcile the journey that brought us to this point with the uncertainty that lies ahead. For me, that question loomed large as I stood on the precipice of change, staring at the path I'd walked within the NFL, wondering if I had done enough or if there was more meant for me elsewhere.

The weight of it all sank in. I had spent years climbing the ladder in a league synonymous with American culture, shaping its internal culture, fostering diversity, and driving equity. But standing in my office, I found myself at a crossroads. Not just the kind where you weigh pros and cons, listing out logical next steps. No, this was about something deeper. It wasn't burnout. It wasn't dissatisfaction. It was something I couldn't quite name. If I wasn't positioned well enough to lead meaningful change here, could it be that my fight was meant to continue somewhere else? Had I reached the ceiling here, or was I being prepared for something else? And if so . . . where?

Just as I began to grapple with this internal dialogue, a new opportunity appeared: a newly created role for Chief Diversity and Inclusion Officer had been posted within the NFL's Human Resources department. This was a first-of-its-kind position at NFL headquarters. This role felt like it had my name on it—a perfect alignment of my professional experiences and personal mission. It was more than just a title. It felt like a calling, a culmination of everything I had been working toward, not just within the NFL, but in life.

The stakes were high. This wasn't just another step on the career ladder; it was the moment I had been waiting for. Doubt began to creep in. Should I take the leap? Should I bet on myself and trust that my skills, my passion, and my work would be enough?

> *Doubt began to creep in. Should I take the leap?*

My work in DEI within the NFL had been intentional, to say the least. From serving on the NFL Diversity Council and co-chairing the Black Engagement Network to managing the Bill Walsh Diversity Coaching Fellowship, my involvement went beyond titles—it was personal. These DEI initiatives weren't part of my official labor relations work portfolio; I had volunteered my time, effort, and attention to them. This work ran parallel to my day-to-day responsibilities in labor operations and labor relations because it mattered—to me, and to the league.

I had poured myself into creating pathways for talent that had been overlooked for too long. I had fought to ensure that voices, particularly those from underrepresented backgrounds, were not just heard but valued.

While I was managing the NFL's diversity coaching fellowship, it blossomed, bringing in diverse coaches and talent that reshaped the way teams thought about their staff. I was responsible for leading the annual Bill Walsh Diversity Coaching Fellowship advisory council meeting during the NFL Scouting Combine in February. This advisory council was made up of a cross-section of NFL head coaches, general managers, team and league office executives, and strategic partners who were committed to diversifying the NFL's coaching pipeline. I used this meeting to not only report on the progress of the league-wide program for that year but also to foster dialogue with council members on how we could innovate and evolve the program to better serve the future of the league.

Through this work, I had earned the trust of head coaches, general managers, and executives at NFL headquarters. My commitment and results had spoken for themselves, and now it seemed like everything was pointing to this moment.

The position of Chief Diversity and Inclusion Officer was two levels above my current position within Labor Operations in the Management Council. It represented a significant jump in both responsibility and leadership within the organization, and was a role that would allow me to not only leverage my past experience but also bring real change—systemic, lasting change. But the question that lingered in the back of my mind was this: Was I ready to take that step? Or worse, would others see me as ready?

It's an internal dialogue so many of us face, especially those who have spent years navigating spaces where we are often the only one who looks like us. Despite the work, despite the results, there's always that voice that whispers, "Are you sure you belong here? Is this really meant for you?" But I knew I couldn't let fear decide for me. Not this time.

After a sleepless night of wrestling with self-doubt and prayer, I chose faith. I reached out to the Senior Vice President of HR to express my interest in the role. My senior leadership at the NFL Management Council believed in me; they encouraged me to go for it, and they promised their support. Yet even with that backing, there was still that lingering question that so many of us carry: Why is it that when we are on the cusp of something significant, doubt creeps in?

The SVP's response to my expressed interest was encouraging. He readily agreed to meet, and that agreement felt like a door opening. The confirmation sparked a sense of purpose within me. This meeting wasn't just another conversation; it was an opportunity to step fully into the work I'd been preparing for all along.

In the days leading up to the meeting, I carried with me a quiet confidence. It wasn't arrogance or over-assurance—it was the belief that my preparation, my experiences, and my calling were converging at this moment for a reason. Surely, I thought, God wouldn't align all these pieces only to close the door now, but as much as I believed that, there was still a small voice of caution. Life is filled with moments where our faith is stretched to its limits. How often do we find ourselves at the brink of something meaningful, only to be tested by the reality that what we think is meant for us might not always be ours?

How do we reconcile that tension? The tension between faith and the reality that sometimes things don't go the way we envisioned? As I mentally prepared for the meeting, these questions hovered in the background, reminding me of the delicate balance between faith, hope, and the unknown.

The day arrived—a sunny Friday afternoon in July. The city felt alive, as if every breath I took on my commute from East Harlem to Midtown carried a weight of expectation. Something about this day felt different, almost like a moment of destiny unfolding. The air, thick with the hum of Manhattan in the summer, seemed charged—not just with the promise of promotion or advancement but with something deeper.

Have you ever experienced the nature of pivotal moments? Even when the signs seem to align in our favor, there's always a part of us that holds back—guarded, quietly preparing for the possibility that things may not go the way we hope. It's that strange duality, where hope meets caution, and ambition meets uncertainty. I felt it, even as I walked into the office building, dressed for the moment, mentally prepared for what I was about to present.

The meeting started with the usual pleasantries. Small talk filled the first few minutes—chatter about the weather, weekend plans— but I was ready to transition the conversation. When the moment came, I took a breath, steadying myself, and then I dove in.

I expressed my interest in the role, laying out my vision for what the Chief Diversity and Inclusion Officer could be, not just for the league but for the culture it influences. As I spoke, I felt the weight of every word. This wasn't just about a new title—it was about stepping into a calling, about using everything I had learned to push the league and the culture forward. I could feel the magnitude of the moment settling over me, the significance of what this role could mean, not just for me, but for the people it was meant to serve.

The SVP leaned back in his chair, nodding thoughtfully. There was a pause, a momentary silence, the kind that makes you question whether the next words will confirm your hopes or dismantle them. His eyes met mine, and then he spoke: "We appreciate all the work you've done in DEI for the league. Once we hire someone for this role, we'll introduce you to them to discuss the possibilities of you supporting their team."

And just like that, everything shifted. His words didn't land softly; they dropped with the weight of finality. *Once we hire someone?* A slow realization crept in, wrapping itself around me. The door I had been pushing open was closing, and I didn't see it coming. The message was clear—I wasn't going to be considered for the role. Yet, it didn't just feel like a rejection. It felt like erasure.

In my mind, I had envisioned the work, the impact, the moment

I'd finally be able to more fully drive change at the highest level. I had imagined what it would feel like to push the league forward through that role in ways that mattered, but in an instant, that vision shattered. I wasn't just passed over. I was never even considered.

> *Why not me?*
> *What more could*
> *I have done?*

Disappointment hit hard, a familiar ache that took me back to moments I thought I had left behind. The sting of feeling unseen, the echo of not being "good enough" rang in my ears, resurfacing old doubts. Childhood insecurities crept back in, whispering the age-old questions: *Why not me? What more could I have done?*

How could this have happened? A role that felt almost divinely orchestrated for me was now slipping through my fingers. I had given so much to the league, poured my heart into every initiative, every project, and yet, here I was, being told, in no uncertain terms, that the opportunity wasn't mine. It was crushing, not just for what it meant professionally, but because it spoke to a deeper narrative that so many of us, particularly those from underrepresented backgrounds, know too well.

We've all faced this struggle. We've been told, in so many ways, that we are not enough—even when we've done everything right. How often do we internalize those messages, allowing them to shape our sense of self-worth, to dictate how we see ourselves in spaces that weren't built with us in mind?

I walked back to my desk, the weight of the moment sinking in. This was more than just a professional setback—it felt personal. I had to sit with the disappointment, wrestle with the reality that, despite all I had done, all I had hoped for, the door had been closed. I was feeling the weight of the unspoken barriers, the silent dismissals that too often leave people feeling unseen and undervalued.

That night, the weight of the day hung heavy on me. I sat down with Brittany, my wife of nearly six years at the time. Brittany wasn't just someone who supported me from the sidelines—she had been in the trenches with me, walking every step of this journey. From the moment we met as undergraduates at the University of Illinois at Urbana-Champaign, she had seen it all: the highs, the lows, the victories, the defeats. Every milestone, every leap of faith, every season of uncertainty—I never faced them alone because Brittany was there, steady and unwavering.

She witnessed it all—the endless hours I poured into building relationships, networking, learning, and serving, and the nights when doubt threatened to overshadow faith. She saw me navigate the world not just with ambition but with a deep trust in God, often walking by faith and not by sight. And because she had seen the fullness of my journey—the good, the bad, the ugly—she had a unique perspective on the shifts and challenges as they unfolded in real time.

As I sat with her that evening, my frustrations spilled out before I could even collect my thoughts. Brittany listened, her quiet presence steadying me in a way only she could. I didn't have to explain everything—she already understood. She always understood. There was a comfort in her knowing, in the way she had this remarkable ability to hold space for my emotions without judgment or impatience. Her love wasn't showy—it was steadfast, like the kind of foundation you don't notice until you realize you've been leaning on it all along.

"It doesn't make sense," I finally said, my voice tinged with exhaustion. "How could something that felt so right slip away like that?"

Brittany nodded, her eyes soft but discerning. "Maybe it's not slipping away. Maybe it's just not the time, or maybe there's something else."

Her words carried weight, not because they diminished my feelings but because they reminded me of something deeper. Brittany had this rare gift of balancing hope with realism. She didn't just offer comfort—she offered perspective. Her response wasn't about dismissing the pain of the moment but about encouraging me to see beyond it.

Isn't that one of the most powerful roles anyone can play in your life? Brittany's presence reminded me of a truth I had always held on to but needed to hear again: Vulnerability builds connection. By being vulnerable with her, I found the strength to keep going, and by being present with me, she reminded me of her own capacity—a capacity that so many women possess—to be a source of unwavering strength for their loved ones. It's a superpower, whether they realize it or not, and Brittany wielded it with quiet grace.

We sat with that thought for a moment, letting it settle between us. It's easy to say "trust the process" when things are going well, when the path ahead is clear and the pieces fall into place. But when the road twists in ways you didn't expect, when the disappointment feels like a wound still fresh, trusting the process seems more like a test of faith than a choice.

But Brittany's presence grounded me. Together, we agreed to trust God's timing, to remain open to whatever His plan might be. It wasn't easy—far from it. How do you find the strength to keep moving forward when the path ahead is blurred with uncertainty? When everything in you wants to retreat, to pull back into the safety of what you know?

I've learned this is where the real test of faith comes in. You must trust in a future you can't see, to believe that the disappointment of today could be setting the stage for something greater tomorrow. As much as I wanted to lean into that belief, it didn't take away the sting of the present. The what-ifs lingered, and as much as I wanted to trust, I knew the journey ahead wouldn't be without its challenges.

Trinity Church NYC, led by pastors Taylor and Kristen Wilkerson, had become more than just a place of worship—it was our refuge. Amid the long workdays and career uncertainties, it was where Brittany and I found our grounding, where we invested ourselves deeply in leadership roles that felt like an extension of our purpose. Every Sunday, from dawn until late afternoon, we served our church community. It wasn't just a duty; it was a calling. Weekly leadership meetings started at 7 a.m., long before the city truly woke up, before Brittany and I would head off to our respective jobs in the private sector. On those Sundays, something shifted. Despite the demanding role I had at the NFL, the ministry tugged at me. Occasionally, I was asked to preach sermons for the senior pastors. Standing at that pulpit, sharing words of faith and hope, I felt a pull that was hard to ignore—a feeling that perhaps there was something more for me beyond the corporate grind. Yet, I juggled both worlds, trusting that God would reveal the right path in His time.

One afternoon, after a particularly long Sunday of service, I found myself chatting with Roger Mason Jr., the former NBA star turned entrepreneur. Roger was a member of our church and attended regularly, and though we had crossed paths a few times before, this conversation felt different—more personal, more grounded in the mutual respect we had for each other's journeys.

As we spoke, I casually mentioned my work with the NFL. Roger's reaction caught me off guard.

"Wait," he said, eyebrows raised in surprise. "You? I thought you worked full-time for the church. Wow, I had no idea."

His surprise reflected something deeper—how fully vested I was in the church community. To him, and maybe to others, it appeared as if my entire life revolved around ministry. In some ways, that assumption wasn't far from the truth. My heart was deeply rooted in serving others through the church, but I was balancing two worlds that, on the surface, seemed disconnected. Yet, somehow, they both felt necessary for this chapter of my life.

It made me think, though. Perhaps I had been so focused on the NFL, on climbing that ladder, that I hadn't fully considered how intertwined my faith and my work had become. Serving at Trinity wasn't just a side pursuit—it was shaping how I saw leadership, community, and purpose. And for the first time, I wondered: Had I been so focused on climbing one ladder that I missed another one forming right beside me? I had spent so much time proving my value in one world that I never stopped to ask if I was meant to be in another. There's something about giving your time and energy to others that shifts your perspective—it reminds you that your worth isn't tied to a job title or the validation of others.

Nevertheless the sting of being passed over for the NFL's Chief Diversity and Inclusion Officer still lingered, and as much as I tried to move forward, that sense of a missed opportunity kept resurfacing. Months passed, and just as I was settling into a rhythm again, I received a call that would test my faith and resilience in a whole new way.

It wasn't unusual for people to reach out for advice or connections, especially given my network within professional sports. My phone would often buzz with requests from former colleagues, mentees, and even friends looking to break into the industry.

A fellow church member reached out and explained that his friend was in the final interview stages for a high-profile position at the NFL, where I worked. "Could you connect with him and offer some insight?" he asked. He hoped that I could perhaps offer advice to help his friend through the final stages of the process. I agreed, ready to lend my usual support and guidance.

As he began describing the role in somewhat vague terms, my

mind started to wander—scanning through my network for potential connections I could introduce him to, thinking through strategies for navigating the final rounds of the hiring process. And then, as I was mapping out how best to support this candidate, he dropped the title: Chief Diversity and Inclusion Officer.

I froze.

The very role I had believed was meant for me—the one I had prayed over, prepared for, and hoped to step into—was now the focus of someone else's final interview.

The timing felt almost cruel, reopening wounds I thought had healed. I sat there, listening, trying to keep my voice steady as the familiar ache of disappointment washed over me. This was the role I had aspired to, the role I believed I was meant for. And yet, here I was, being asked to help someone else secure it.

"I'm happy to help," I said, though every part of me wanted to scream.

I took a deep breath, reminding myself of a principle I'd long held on to: "You only make a living by what you get, but you make a life by what you give." I chose to support this candidate just as I would any other, leaning into the belief that what is meant for me will always be for me.

When I finally spoke with the candidate, I was struck by his preparedness. He was incredibly smart, having spent a stint in my hometown of Chicago for grad school at the University of Chicago, and was serving in an executive leadership role at one of the world's top consulting firms. We connected over shared values—particularly our faith-centered approach to leadership and our deep commitment to diversity, equity, and inclusion.

As we talked, I felt the weight of my emotions lifting, even if only slightly. This was someone I genuinely wanted to help succeed. Still, I couldn't help but wonder—Would there be space for me in his vision? Could there be a way forward that included us both?

The NFL leadership ultimately decided to only engage him as a consultant, rather than a full-time employee. He ended up moving on from the opportunity and stayed with his consulting firm, and the role—at least as I had imagined it—seemed to vanish, with no one ultimately filling the position at that time. Tuck this point away in your memory, as we'll return to it later in our journey.

By April 2019, my focus had shifted entirely to the fast-approaching NFL draft, one of the league's most anticipated events. The NFL draft had evolved from a modest gathering into a multiday spectacle, drawing record-breaking crowds and millions of viewers. It was an exciting, high-pressure environment, and my role had grown significantly over the years. I had been enlisted by the head of the NFL Player Personnel department to work alongside him at the draft head table. I would be responsible for managing the trade phones and trade desks, handling some of the most critical moments of the draft.

The draft itself was a finely tuned operation, an intricate dance between team executives, coaches, and the league office. Teams could negotiate trades at any time during the draft, whether it was to move up for a coveted player or to improve their position for future drafts. When two teams agreed to a trade, both would call the head table—where the head of NFL Player Personnel and I sat—to confirm the details. The trade would be approved only when both clubs relayed the same information. From there, the details would be passed along to all thirty-two clubs and the league's broadcast partners. It was my job to ensure that everything flowed smoothly and that trades were accurately recorded during live television.

I had to be prepared for anything, and as the day approached, I was singularly focused on the task ahead. There was no room for distraction.

I was ready to head to Nashville for the draft when Brittany stopped me just before I left for the airport. Her friend and former colleague from Hillary Clinton's 2016 presidential campaign had just been hired as the Chief Operating Officer for Joe Biden's newly announced presidential campaign. Biden's campaign was gaining momentum, and the energy surrounding it was already palpable. Brittany's friend had reached out to see if she would join the campaign staff, but after her work on Clinton's CFO team, led by Gary Gensler, who would later become chairman of the SEC, she was ready for a different path. She politely declined.

As the call was about to wrap up, her friend mentioned that the campaign was also looking to hire a Chief People Officer and Head of Diversity and Inclusion. He asked if Brittany knew anyone suitable for the role, which would involve building the HR infrastructure and leading the campaign's DEI efforts.

At the time, I was entirely focused on the NFL and the upcoming draft. My dream had always been to work my way up to NFL team president or, one day, commissioner. If opportunities didn't align with that vision, I wasn't interested. When Brittany asked if I knew anyone who might be a good fit, something inside me stirred. It was subtle, almost like a whisper, but it was clear: "Your dream? So, you're not willing to serve now?"

I paused, contemplating the moment. *Well, it can't hurt to be connected with the campaign*, I thought. After all, this wasn't just any campaign—it was for the former vice president of the United States under the first-ever Black president. I told Brittany to let her friend know I was interested in learning more about the role and would be happy to set up a call after the draft.

The week following the draft, I was back at NFL headquarters, diving into the postdraft whirlwind of catching up on work and other tasks that had piled up while I was out in Nashville. It was late in the evening when an email from Biden's presidential campaign COO landed in my inbox. He wanted to set up a call to discuss the Chief People Officer and Head of Diversity and Inclusion role. Most of my colleagues had already left for the day, so I took a deep breath and replied that I was available for an impromptu conversation.

As the call connected, the COO's voice carried an urgency that immediately piqued my interest. He described the magnitude of the campaign and the critical need to build out the HR infrastructure. This wasn't just about managing people—it was about leading the organizational culture for a presidential campaign that had the potential to reshape the country's future. The role would involve overseeing all HR functions, from talent acquisition to organizational development, and most important, driving the campaign's diversity, equity, and inclusion strategy.

As he outlined the job, I found myself mentally reviewing my network—thinking of who might be a strong fit for this high-profile role. Midthought, the COO interrupted my brainstorming: "I appreciate you thinking through potential candidates," he said, "but I've been following your journey, particularly through Brittany's updates on social media. Your background in labor operations, organizational culture, and your ability to connect with people is exactly what we need. I envision you in this role. What do you think?"

For a moment, I was stunned. This was the kind of opportunity I hadn't even realized I was looking for—an intersection of my professional skill set and my deeper calling to serve and lead. It was also a world I knew little about. I had never worked in politics, never been on a campaign, and certainly never thought I'd be in a position to shape the HR infrastructure for a presidential bid. Could this really be the next step in my journey?

Then, as clear as anything I've ever heard, God's voice pierced through the noise of my racing thoughts: *This is it*. It wasn't just a whisper; it was a declaration. A moment of undeniable clarity. The words settled in my soul, anchoring me in the certainty that this was not just another opportunity. This was a calling. God was redirecting my path in a way I couldn't have foreseen, and in that moment, everything seemed to shift.

"Let me think about it," I said carefully, wanting to give the decision the consideration it deserved. But deep down, the answer was already written. As I hung up the phone, I sat in the quiet conference room at NFL HQ, letting the weight of that moment wash over me. This was it. The path was unfolding before me, and it was time to step forward in faith.

Over the next few days, the weight of the decision didn't leave me. Brittany and I had countless conversations, praying for clarity and guidance. She reminded me that every time we had leapt into the unknown before, God had met us there. But this felt different. The NFL wasn't just a job, it was part of who I was, something I had built and nurtured for nearly a decade. Walking away felt like letting go of a piece of myself.

Still, the pull was undeniable. The timing. The opportunity. The still, small voice whispering, *This is where you're meant to be*—it all seemed to align. Was I more attached to the title and role I had built than to the assignment God was calling me toward?

Brittany and I spent hours mapping out the realities of such a move. A campaign role offered nothing close to the stability I had in the NFL. We reviewed financials, contingency plans, worst-case scenarios—everything. The uncertainty was unnerving. And yet, beneath the nerves, there was an unexpected sense of peace—a reminder that even when the weight of a decision won't leave you, neither will God.

That peace—that quiet reassurance that stepping into the unknown might actually be the right move—was something I couldn't ignore. Even as I continued with my responsibilities at NFL HQ, the decision weighed on me. I knew I had to face it head-on and prepare for what could be one of the biggest shifts in my career.

The thought of resigning from the NFL felt surreal. I had grown so much within the league—navigating labor operations, labor relations, and even DEI initiatives, all while building relationships with top executives and earning their respect. To leave that behind was a risk, but as I spent time in prayer and reflection, I realized something important: God doesn't always call us to stay in the comfortable spaces where we've succeeded. Sometimes He calls us to step into something new, something unknown, because that's where the next level of growth lies.

A Leap of Faith

The decision to leave the NFL came in waves—a series of confirmations, moments of clarity, and occasional doubts. But once the commitment was made, it felt like everything shifted. I could sense the gravity of the step I was about to take. It wasn't just about leaving the comfort of a stable career; it was about stepping into a new realm of influence, responsibility, and unknown challenges. As I prepared to make my resignation official, there were moments where I found myself second-guessing. The weight of the unknown loomed large. What if this move didn't lead to anything concrete? What if I was stepping away from the NFL just as more opportunities were opening up for me? But the voice inside me— the one that said, *This is it*—was louder than my fear.

I knew this wasn't just a professional transition; it was a spiritual one. God was calling me to something higher, something that required me to relinquish the comfort of my plans and embrace His. The NFL had shaped me, but it wasn't my ultimate destination and that much was clear now.

Brittany, in her usual supportive manner, reminded me that God's timing is perfect. She always had a way of grounding me in moments like these. Together, we reaffirmed our faith that this decision, though risky, was right. It was in line with the values we had built our lives upon—faith, purpose, and service.

This decision was also about something greater than us. The country was at a crossroads. Morale was low, divisions were high, and a deep sense of unease seemed to hang in the air. We were grappling with rising tensions around race, inequality, and justice, all set against the backdrop of growing polarization. The rhetoric that filled the national conversation felt heavier by the day, feeding into fear and uncertainty. Yet, even in that heaviness, there was a flicker of something else—a hunger for leadership that would inspire hope, unify communities, and work toward healing the fractures in our collective identity.

To step into this moment alongside Joe Biden, the former vice president to the nation's first Black president, felt deeply symbolic. It was more than a political opportunity—it was a chance to contribute to a moment that could restore faith in what America could be. I felt the weight of that responsibility, but I also felt the call to meet it. This wasn't just about the logistics of building an HR infrastructure or shaping DEI strategies; it was about helping to lay the foundation for a movement that could bring people together in pursuit of a shared purpose. The work ahead wouldn't be easy, but it would be necessary—and deeply meaningful.

I believed that even small contributions could help shift the tide. It was a chance to pour hope into a nation desperate for it. I couldn't ignore the pull in my spirit—a sense that this was part of something far bigger than myself. It wasn't just a career move; it was an answer to the higher call of service, a step into a purpose I hadn't fully imagined but knew I was being prepared for. Stepping into a new chapter meant closing an old one, and that wasn't easy.

I arranged a meeting with the head of Labor Operations at the NFL. He had been more than just a boss—he was a mentor, someone who saw the potential in others and made it his mission to help them grow. His leadership wasn't about merely recognizing talent; it was about cultivating it with intention. He had a remarkable ability to look beyond surface impressions and focus on helping his team members become the best versions of themselves.

I walked into his office, my heart pounding with a mix of excitement and trepidation. This was it—the moment I would officially step away from the NFL. As I sat down, I could feel the weight of the moment. I was about to announce a decision that would change everything.

"Peter, I want to express my deepest gratitude for the opportunity to work under your leadership," I began. "I've learned so much and grown in ways I never imagined, but I feel it's time for me to pursue a new path."

Peter listened carefully, nodding as I spoke. When I finished, he leaned back in his chair, absorbing my words. After a moment, he smiled. "I've always known you would be great leading HR, Michael. You're going to do great things. Congratulations on this next chapter."

His response was everything I needed in that moment. It was both a validation of my decision and a reminder that I had built something here—something I could carry with me as I moved forward.

We discussed the logistics of my transition, how I would inform the rest of the team, and what my departure would mean for the department. Peter's support and encouragement were a balm to the weight of anxiety I had been shouldering. It was clear that he understood this was more than just a career move for me. It was a step into the unknown, guided by faith and purpose.

As I left his office, I felt a wave of relief wash over me. The decision had been made, and the path ahead, while uncertain, was now in motion.

My resignation date was set for Wednesday, June 19, 2019—Juneteenth. Was it a coincidence? Perhaps—or more likely, it was God's providence. The significance of that day, a day marking the emancipation of enslaved African Americans, now marked my own step toward freedom. Not freedom from oppression, but from a career that, while deeply rewarding at times, no longer aligned with where God was calling me to be. I saw it as a divine nod, a signal that this was part of a larger narrative—one that extended beyond my own ambitions.

Joe Biden's campaign had officially launched just a month and a half earlier, and they were eager for me to join as soon as possible. The leadership team wanted me to build out the HR infrastructure and lead the campaign's strategic efforts in diversity, equity, and inclusion. As I prepared to leave the NFL—a place I had poured so much of myself into—I was stepping into uncharted territory. I knew my faith, my skills, and my passion would be tested in ways I couldn't foresee.

In the days leading up to my first day on the Biden campaign, I was caught between two worlds. On one hand, the NFL—a place that had defined nearly a decade of my life, a place where I had grown professionally and personally. On the other, politics—a world I had never been a part of, yet a world where the stakes were higher than ever before. As I packed up my office and walked out for the last time, the weight of the moment settled in. This wasn't just about leaving a job; it was about walking into something far bigger than myself.

Brittany and I spent countless hours in prayer and conversation about what this new chapter would mean for us. The life of a political campaign was entirely different from the structured world we knew in New York City and the NFL. Campaigns were grueling, unpredictable, and intense. They required long hours and sacrifices we hadn't yet fully grasped. We knew that living apart for extended periods would test us, but the more we talked about it, the clearer it became that this was where God was leading me.

The Next Step

On June 20, the day after I officially resigned from the NFL, I began my new journey on the Biden campaign. The shift was immediate and profound. The frenetic pace of a political campaign was unlike anything I had experienced before. The stakes were higher, the energy was different, and there was a sense of urgency that was palpable in every decision, every move.

This was more than just work. This was about stepping into a moment that could shape the future of the country. I had to remind myself, again and again, that God had brought me here for a reason. My role was clear: I was there to build the HR infrastructure, to create a culture of diversity, equity, and inclusion—values that had always been core to who I was but now were front and center in a high-stakes political landscape.

The learning curve was steep. I had to get up to speed quickly, understand the dynamics of the campaign, and figure out how to make an immediate impact. The skills I had honed over my career—the ability to build relationships, foster trust, and lead with purpose—were exactly what I needed to navigate this new terrain. As the days went on, I found my footing, but I also knew this was just the beginning.

I was walking into the unknown with nothing but faith—and it felt right.

CHAPTER 5

Leaping from Stability
to Uncertainty

THERE'S SOMETHING ABOUT THE MOMENT YOU LEAP INTO the unknown. It's exhilarating, terrifying, and freeing all at once. There's no easing into it. No gentle transition. It's a plunge.

Every leap of faith requires you to let go of the familiar. It forces you to surrender the comfort of what you know in exchange for the possibility of something greater. The question is, are you willing to trust that the leap will take you where you're meant to go?

The Biden campaign wasn't just another job. It was a call to step into something far bigger than myself. The stakes were enormous because it was a campaign that could change the course of history. The Democratic primary field was crowded, with more than twenty candidates vying for the nomination. Bernie Sanders, Elizabeth Warren, Kamala Harris, Pete Buttigieg, Cory Booker, just to name a few—all formidable opponents. Joe Biden wasn't even the frontrunner when I joined the campaign.

That's the thing about walking by faith. You don't always see the destination clearly. You just know you're being called to move forward.

In the early days, one document became incredibly helpful to my work: "#CampaignEquity: A Blueprint for Safety, Inclusion, and Equity in Political Campaign Work." Born from lessons of past campaigns, especially Bernie Sanders's 2016 effort, this wasn't just a manual—it was a declaration. Its guiding principles were clear: "Your People Are Your Key to Victory" and "Your Campaign Culture Should Align with Your Campaign Values." These words echoed a deeper truth: This wasn't just about policy; it was about people. If we didn't take care of our own team, how could we possibly hope to lead a nation in need of healing?

This wasn't theoretical. It was practical. These principles were a framework to build something lasting—a culture where every voice mattered, every person felt valued. And in the chaotic, high-stakes world of politics, that was no small feat. I leaned into this document as a blueprint not just for operational success but for the soul of the campaign.

Saying yes to the campaign was more than a professional decision—it was a personal one. It meant stepping into a world where division often ruled, a world that was a stark contrast to the camaraderie of the NFL. And it meant sacrificing time with my family, particularly with Brittany.

I remember the looks and the side comments. Some friends, even family, couldn't understand why I would leave a stable career for something so uncertain—something with an expiration date. To them, it felt like madness. To me, it felt like faith.

How often do we let others' fears shape our decisions? Their doubts, their worries—they seep in, often disguised as care. I was learning that faith isn't about what makes sense to others. It's about trusting what God has placed inside of you, even when the world tells you otherwise.

Brittany and I leaned on our faith more than ever. This wasn't just about the campaign or the job, it was about a higher calling. We believed this season of sacrifice would birth something greater. We were tested, not just by the miles that separated us, but by the weight of the moment.

===

Walking into Biden's campaign headquarters was like entering another world. Gone were the gleaming, billion-dollar facilities of the NFL. In their place was a sparse, scrappy operation—where urgency was the air we breathed, and every decision felt like a life-or-death moment. This was politics. A world where the stakes weren't just games or contracts—they were the soul of the nation.

Imagine stepping onto a battlefield with unfamiliar terrain. The rules you've lived by don't apply here. There's no playbook, no polished systems. It's chaotic, unpredictable, and in that chaos, you have to find your footing or be swept away.

In those early days, I made it my mission to listen and learn. I met with as many people as I could—absorbing the culture, the dynamics, the challenges that lay ahead. I reminded myself that the lessons from the NFL still held weight. Discipline, structure, and strategy were still relevant, but the political arena required something deeper. It demanded a connection to the ideals we were fighting for: unity, justice, restoring the soul of a divided nation.

I would be lying if I said doubt didn't creep in. There were days when I wondered if I had made the right choice, if I was out of my depth. Then I'd remember why I was here. It wasn't about me—it was about something bigger and that kept me moving forward.

Despite my best efforts, there were times when I felt like I was on an island. The campaign was fast-paced and demanding, and I often found myself alone, managing the entire HR function without a single support staff or team member. Other senior leaders seemed to have an easier time securing the resources they needed, while I was left to navigate a mountain of responsibilities on my own. The isolation was real, and it weighed heavily on me, especially when the COO who had hired me parted ways with the campaign. It felt like the one lifeline I had was ripped away, and I was unsure of what would come next. The fear that I might be pushed out or undermined gnawed at me in the quiet hours of the night.

When I needed it most, Maju Varghese stepped in. I didn't know him personally, but his reputation preceded him. He had been hired as the new COO, the very person I would now be reporting to on a day-to-day basis. Brought in by the campaign manager, Maju was a veteran of the Obama White House and earlier presidential campaign bids. When we finally sat down together, I briefed him on everything that had been transpiring and explained the immense challenges I was facing, particularly the fact that I had been leading the entire HR function alone. Maju listened intently and he didn't just empathize, he acted. He understood the pressures and complexities of a campaign at this level, and he worked tirelessly to ensure that I had the support and resources I needed to succeed. With his backing, I began to find my footing again.

Soon Myra Caesar, a Black woman and US Army veteran with two decades of HR experience, joined our team. Together, we began building something solid—a team that reflected the very values we were fighting for. It wasn't about ticking diversity boxes. It was about creating an environment where everyone felt empowered, valued, and seen, while carrying out the operations and HR functions of the campaign with excellence.

The Storm Intensifies: COVID-19 and George Floyd

As the COVID-19 pandemic escalated, we knew we had to pivot—fast. On the same day that we were set to announce a fully remote campaign operations shift for the foreseeable future, we were also preparing to inform the team about a significant leadership change: a new campaign manager. There was no easing into it. The moment demanded swift adaptation, and the stakes couldn't have been higher.

The logistical nightmare of moving a national campaign to remote operations was one thing, but then, May 25, 2020, happened.

George Floyd, a forty-six-year-old Black man, was murdered by police in broad daylight in Minneapolis. It was an image, a sound, a cry for humanity that pierced through the fog of everything else. The video of Floyd pinned beneath the knee of a white police officer, Derek Chauvin, for nine agonizing minutes and twenty-nine seconds shook the world.

I remember the moment the news broke. It felt like a gut punch—a weight pressing down on my chest, familiar but no less devastating. "I can't breathe," Floyd pleaded over and over. His voice trembled, calling out for his mother in his final moments, a desperate cry that echoed the pain, fear, and helplessness of Black people everywhere.

I sat in stunned silence, my heart racing, my mind trying to comprehend the depth of what I had just witnessed. George Floyd could have been me. He could have been my brother, my father, my friend. This wasn't just another tragedy. It was an unrelenting reminder of the trauma Black Americans had been enduring for generations. The stark reality of systemic racism wasn't theoretical—it was happening, and it was happening again.

This wasn't just another news story. This was a moment—a reckoning. Protests erupted across the nation, and the world took notice. People poured into the streets, demanding justice, demanding change, demanding that the very foundations of inequality be torn down.

Within hours of the news, my dear friend and colleague called me. We both knew that we had to act. This wasn't just about campaign strategy anymore. This was about healing, about acknowledging the pain and trauma that Black staff—that all of us—

> *This was a moment— a reckoning.*

were feeling. We needed to bring our campaign family together, to create space for our Black staff to be seen, heard, and valued in a way that George Floyd had been denied.

Our campaign manager began the call, acknowledging the weight of the moment. We needed to create a space for truth, vulnerability, and collective healing. Joe Biden and Dr. Jill Biden offered words of comfort and unity, pledging to fight for the civil and human rights that George Floyd had been denied. Their words were heartfelt and so very needed by everyone on that Zoom call.

Then, it was my turn. I was tasked with leading the rest of the session—a session that felt, in many ways, like the most important moment of the campaign. It wasn't just a conversation; it was a reckoning. I knew that the words I spoke in this moment would either bring us closer together or risk leaving us more fragmented.

I began by leveling with our staff, explaining how we intended to use this time to reflect, to share, and to try and start the process of healing. "Today, we're going to take a moment to breathe," I said, my voice steady but heavy with emotion. "We're going to reflect. We're going to share." I spoke about how painful it had been to witness George Floyd's murder, and how, as a Black man, the images brought back memories of my own experiences with law enforcement.

I shared the story of my first-ever experience being pulled over by the police, a moment etched into my memory from my teenage years. It happened on my way to a Wednesday night church service. At first, it seemed like a routine traffic stop, but as the encounter unfolded the tension in the air became palpable. The officers asked me to step out of the car. Hands on the hood, I complied, heart pounding as they began to search my vehicle without explanation. I had no idea what I had done wrong, and the fear of making one wrong move caused my heart to race. As I stood with my hands on the hood, I heard the crunch of gravel behind me—what had been one police car had now turned into two.

As the officers rifled through my car, I stood there in silence, feeling the weight of their scrutiny. Then came the demand for proof of insurance. My heart sank. I had neglected to place the new insurance card, which had arrived in the mail, inside my car. The only card I had on me was expired by a week. Anxiety coursed through me as I tried to explain the situation, but they weren't interested in hearing excuses. I pleaded with them, asking for permission to call my father. He could verify that the insurance was active, even if I didn't have the card on hand.

The officers hesitated but finally allowed me to make the call. My dad answered immediately, and I quickly put him on speaker. As my father asked the officers what I had done wrong, I braced myself for their answer. That's when they revealed the reason: the tree-shaped air freshener hanging from my rearview mirror. An obstruction to the driver's view, they claimed.

I was stunned. After all that—the fear, the search, the humiliation—that was their reason for pulling me over? It felt like a slap in the face, a harsh reminder of the scrutiny I would face as a Black man in America. As I shared that story on the campaign's all-staff call, the memory of that moment resurfaced, hitting me with the same intensity as when it first happened.

I invited my colleagues—particularly the Black campaign staff—to share their own stories. What followed was an outpouring of emotion, a moment of raw vulnerability that I had never seen on a professional call before. Staff members shared stories of their own encounters with racism, with injustice, with the unspoken fear that follows so many of us who are Black in America. As they spoke, I could see the Zoom tiles fill with nods, with tears, with the weight of it all being acknowledged in real time.

This wasn't just a staff call. This was a moment of collective mourning, a shared understanding that the system had failed us, again and again. But it was also a call to action—a reminder that the fight for justice wasn't over, and that we, as a campaign, had a responsibility to lead that fight. We ended the call with a renewed sense of purpose. This was just the beginning. This wasn't a time to stop but a time to press forward, together, in unity. The road ahead would not be easy, but we had to keep moving. We had to keep fighting. We had to keep breathing.

That day, the George Floyd murder wasn't just another tragic event in a long line of injustices. It was a mirror, forcing us to confront the gap between American ideals and American realities. It forced us to ask ourselves: How do we lead in a moment when the world feels so divided? How do we create spaces where people feel seen, heard, and valued?

In the days that followed, I held on to one simple truth: Storytelling is a powerful tool. It connects us in ways that nothing else can. In moments of pain, in moments of division, in moments of confusion, it is the sharing of our stories that allows us to see one another—not as distant figures or abstract ideas, but as human beings with real fears, real struggles, and real hopes.

That was what we had done on that call—we had shared our

stories. We had come together, not just as a campaign team, but as people. And in doing so, we had breathed life into one another in a moment when the world seemed intent on taking our breath away.

The pandemic had grown so severe in New York that Brittany and I decided she should join me in Philadelphia. She moved into my tiny four-hundred-square-foot apartment, and we both worked full-time from the small space. The strain of the situation was intense. We coordinated and alternated our virtual meetings, often finding ourselves working from corners of the studio or even the bathroom to maintain some semblance of privacy. The walls seemed to close in on us, and the weight of the world outside seeped into our small space.

One night, as the protests grew more violent and the smell of smoke filled our apartment, I became deeply concerned for our safety. Philadelphia and the surrounding areas where we were located had deteriorated rapidly. Violence and looting sprang up in numerous neighborhoods across the city, as protesters outnumbered city and state police. The National Guard had been deployed to Philadelphia to help restore order, but frightening confrontations continued to erupt, leaving us uncertain about what might happen next. The constant sirens, the shouts from the streets, and the increasing tension weighed heavily on my mind. I booked the next available flight to the South Suburbs of Chicago, where our parents lived. It was safer, quieter, and more conducive to our mental health; even in that relative safety, the emotional toll was undeniable. The weight of the world felt like it was crushing down on us, and I began to realize that I was nearing a breaking point.

There were no boundaries between work and life—our world had become a constant blur of Zoom calls, emails, and crises. The isolation of the pandemic, the relentless pressure of the campaign, and the ever-present weight of social unrest had all converged, leaving me feeling depleted.

I knew something had to change. I couldn't continue pouring from an empty cup.

After Brittany and I had made it safely to the Chicago suburbs, I reached out to Pastor Rich Wilkerson, who had been my pastor during my time in Miami—some of the most formative moments of my life. We talked for nearly an hour, as I felt like I was on the verge of a mental and emotional breakdown. Pastor Rich prayed over me, reminding me that even in the midst of chaos, God was with me. That prayer felt like a lifeline. I didn't have to carry everything on my own. I didn't have to have all the answers. It was okay to let go and trust that God was still in control.

I had also reached out to my younger brother, Martell, whose calm words reminded me to stay the course—teaching me that younger siblings often have wisdom just as valuable as our own. And then, there was my dad, who had always referred to me as a "champion," reminding me that as long as I did my best, God would figure out the rest.

As long as I did my best, God would figure out the rest.

Their words, along with that prayer, gave me the strength I needed to keep moving forward.

The next day, buoyed by their encouragement, I had a conversation with the campaign's COO, Maju, about how I had been feeling. It was one of the most honest and vulnerable conversations I'd had since joining the campaign. I told him how difficult it had been leading the HR and DEI efforts without an adequately sized team, and how the weight of supporting staff through these traumatic moments had taken a toll on me. He listened with empathy and assured me that I wasn't alone. He promised to provide the support I needed to continue leading effectively, and for the first time in a long time, I felt seen.

Then an unexpected email came from the campaign manager, Jen O'Malley Dillon. Jen thanked me for the work I had been doing and shared that both she and Joe Biden were deeply appreciative of my efforts. It was a small gesture, but it meant everything. In that moment, I was reminded that the work I was doing wasn't in vain. It mattered.

Sometimes it takes hitting the edge of your capacity to realize how much you've been carrying. It takes breaking down to understand the importance of building yourself back up, and that's what I began to do—rebuild. Slowly, intentionally, I started taking the time to prioritize my own mental health. I leaned on God, on my family, and on my community. I realized that while the mission of the campaign was important, my well-being was just as essential to seeing it through.

With that clarity, I found the strength to keep moving forward. The campaign wasn't just about electing a president. It was about restoring hope, rebuilding trust, and fighting for the soul of a nation. I knew that in order to continue leading, I had to be in a place of strength, not just for the team but for myself.

====

With renewed clarity and strength, I continued to persevere the best way I knew how. As we continued adjusting to the relentless pace of campaigning during a pandemic, the world continued to shift under our feet. The dual crises of COVID-19 and the battle for social justice were inescapable. The entire nation felt like it was holding its breath, waiting for the next upheaval.

The murder of George Floyd had ignited a firestorm, but it was far from the only injustice. Breonna Taylor, Ahmaud Arbery, Rayshard Brooks, Elijah McClain—the names kept coming, and each one felt like a fresh wound. We couldn't escape the gravity of what was happening around us. As leaders, we were responsible for keeping the team motivated and pushing forward, even as the weight of these injustices bore down on us all.

Campaign life, in its nature, is demanding—long hours, constant strategy adjustments, and a focus on the task at hand. The intersection of the pandemic and the growing social justice movement added an entirely new layer of complexity. Every day, we were balancing the work of getting Joe Biden elected with the very real emotional toll these crises were taking on our team. How do you expect people to focus when the world outside is in chaos? When the next news alert could bring yet another tragedy?

As the Chief People Officer and Head of Diversity and Inclusion, I carried the weight of these dual crises in a unique way. Not only was I responsible for helping ensure that our campaign team functioned effectively, but I was also tasked with supporting staff through the emotional turmoil that had become a daily reality. Every new act of violence, every rise in COVID cases, added layers of pressure. I found myself sending emails to the staff after each tragedy, offering words of encouragement, resources, and space for them to process what was happening. It was necessary, but it was also deeply draining. Each message served as a reminder of how broken our systems were and how much work lay ahead. As I poured into others, creating spaces where people felt heard and supported, I began to realize the emotional toll it was taking on me. Leadership, especially in moments of crisis, often requires a level of emotional labor that can be isolating. The countless lives lost during this time period—to the pandemic and to the ongoing unjust killings—weighed heavily on my spirit, leaving me to navigate the tension between supporting others while neglecting my own needs.

But it wasn't just me. I knew that our staff, particularly those from marginalized backgrounds, were struggling under the weight of these twin crises. They weren't just campaign staff—they were human beings grappling with the very issues we were fighting to address. The campaign had become a mirror, reflecting the broader struggles of the country, and we had to be intentional about how we responded to both the internal and external pressures.

The weight of the world was undeniable, but even amid the turbulence, there were moments of clarity—glimpses of hope. One such moment came when we hit a significant milestone. Despite everything we had been navigating, our campaign had finally built something we could be proud of. As the months of preparation for the general election unfolded, we had assembled the most diverse general election campaign staff in US history. This wasn't just a bullet point or a statistic; it was the embodiment of Joe Biden's values—our values. It was proof that we were not only campaigning for a more inclusive and just nation but that we were living those principles every day. Our team was reflective of America's true diversity, and that was something worth celebrating.

This milestone was a bright spot in the storm. It reminded me of why we were doing this work and what we were fighting for. We were building something bigger than ourselves—something that, for many of us, was personal. And as much as I felt the weariness of the moment, this achievement breathed new life into me. We weren't just talking about change. We were living it, leading it, and embodying it in the very fabric of our campaign.

There were still days when the weight felt heavy, but I continued to lean into the support of my faith and family more than ever. They had been my rock through it all, reminding me that I didn't have to carry this burden alone. I carved out intentional time to seek God each morning, grounding myself before the chaos of the day took over. Slowly, I started to feel the weight lift, piece by piece. I had always known that strength comes not from pushing through exhaustion but from knowing when to rest, when to reset, and when to rely on others.

This journey wasn't just about pushing through—it was about learning to care for myself in the process. And as I did, I became more effective in leading, more present in the moments that mattered. It was as if, by taking care of my own well-being, I was able to pour even more into the mission we were fighting for. We were approaching one of the most consequential elections of our lifetimes, and the stakes couldn't have been higher. I knew that in order for us to reach that finish line, I had to come from a place of strength. This wasn't just about electing a president; it was about restoring hope, rebuilding trust, and bringing the soul of this nation back to life.

Elections and Their Echoes: A Moment of Triumph, Setback, and Reflection

Election Day came and went, but the results didn't come right away. As the nation held its breath, so did we. Every passing hour felt like an eternity, with no clear end in sight. All the work we had put in—the months of building, growing, canvassing, phone banking, and leading—had led us to this moment. Now, all we could do was wait.

But this election was unlike any other. The pandemic had transformed how people voted, with unprecedented numbers of mail-in ballots and early voting. The very fabric of our democracy was being tested, and the outcome felt uncertain. It wasn't just the usual Election Day tension—it was a sense that the country was standing at a crossroads, and the stakes had never been higher.

As we waited for the results, I found myself reflecting on everything it had taken to get to this point. The personal sacrifices, the sleepless nights, the tough decisions—it had all come down to this. We had given everything we had, leaving it all on the field. And now, it was out of our hands.

In those long, uncertain hours, I prayed. Not just for victory, but for the future of our country. This election wasn't just about winning; it was about restoring the soul of the nation, about bringing people together in the face of division. I prayed for unity, for healing, and for the strength to move forward, no matter the outcome.

And then, on November 7, 2020, the news broke. Joe Biden was declared the winner of the presidential election by the Associated Press and major media outlets. I'll never forget that moment. It was as if the entire nation exhaled all at once—a collective sigh of relief. The weight that had been pressing down on us for months was finally lifted.

Across the country, people poured into the streets, celebrating, honking car horns, and waving flags. There was joy, but there was also reflection. We had won, but the work was far from over. The challenges we faced as a nation—racial injustice, economic inequality, a raging pandemic—didn't disappear with the announcement of a victory. If anything, they became even more pressing.

As I stood there, absorbing the moment, I couldn't help but feel both triumph and humility. We had been part of something bigger than ourselves. This wasn't just about politics—it was about the power of faith, resilience, and the belief that change was possible.

Yes, we had won the election, but now came the hard part. How do we govern a divided country? How do we turn the ideals of progress into concrete, tangible realities? How do we heal the wounds that have been festering for so long?

This moment of triumph also held a quiet reminder: Progress is not permanent. Four years later, in 2024, the results of the presidential election told a different story. It was a sobering reality that the path forward is not always straightforward. Sometimes it demands navigating winding roads where clarity feels elusive and the destination uncertain.

During the 2024 campaign, I remember sharing with a senior leader on the Harris for President campaign staff that elections are won not simply with stats but with stories. Early in the campaign, Democrats often emphasized results and policy achievements—over-indexing on accomplishments that were undoubtedly significant but at times disconnected from the personal stories that make those stats come alive. "You can give people the facts," I said, "but if they can't see themselves in the story those facts tell, the connection is lost." It wasn't just about policies—it was about painting a vision of possibility, about helping people feel the human impact of those stats.

Kamala Harris's campaign was a testament to resilience, intellect, and determination. Her ability to lead with grace under immense pressure was nothing short of remarkable. However, the power of storytelling—a lesson deeply ingrained in every campaign—played a pivotal role in shaping the outcome. Both campaigns understood the significance of narrative, but the Republican strategy leaned heavily into stories that, while curated and often rooted in fear, struck a chord with their base. Democrats, on the other hand, while emphasizing results and policies more often than stories, sometimes struggled to close the gap between facts and felt experiences. It was a reminder that facts alone rarely inspire action; it's the stories that connect those facts to people's lives that ultimately move them.

The endorsements from cultural icons like Michelle Obama, Oprah Winfrey, Beyoncé, and Taylor Swift served as powerful symbols of support, but they underscored a broader lesson: Influence alone does not guarantee action. The act of mobilizing people to vote—the gap between knowing and doing—remained a persistent challenge. And while those endorsements carried immense influence, they served as a poignant reminder: Winning endorsements doesn't always translate to winning elections.

The power of connection—garnering more people than your opponent to see themselves in the story—is what ultimately drives action. Campaigns, leadership, and even personal endeavors thrive when people can feel their place in the vision being shared. This lesson extended beyond any single campaign: Listening, storytelling, and intentional succession planning aren't just strategies—they are the foundations of leadership that inspire lasting change. They are bridges, ensuring history doesn't repeat itself, cycle after cycle.

For me, standing in the glow of the 2020 victory, I realized that moments of triumph and setback are part of the same journey. The leap I had taken from the NFL to the Biden campaign wasn't just about stepping into the unknown—it was about choosing faith over fear, believing that every step, whether it leads to victory or challenge, is part of something greater.

As we celebrated that night in 2020, I couldn't have imagined what the future would hold, but I knew then, as I know now, that the work of bridging ideals and realities is not a single moment—it's a lifetime commitment. The journey ahead wouldn't be easy, but it would always be worth it.

Here's the truth about change: It isn't secured in a single election or a moment of triumph. Democracy is an ongoing experiment, constantly tested by shifts in power, societal challenges, and the choices we make to protect or erode progress. Leadership, I realized, isn't about ensuring that nothing changes after you leave—it's about ensuring that what truly matters can endure when everything does.

The key isn't permanence—it's resilience. Resilience in the people we empower, the principles we uphold, and the ability to adapt when systems falter or are dismantled. Because they will be. Disruptions are inevitable in democracy, but resilience isn't about avoiding them—it's about enduring and adapting through them. The path will be uncertain, the progress fragile, but that's the price of any meaningful endeavor. What I learned standing on that precipice between victory and uncertainty is that progress is possible only if we recognize its fragility—and prepare for it.

As I planned for what lay ahead—transitioning from a campaign victory to the unknown—I understood that success wouldn't be measured by what we accomplished in a single administration. It would be measured by how well we prepared others to continue the work, long after our time had passed.

With that understanding and in that spirit, I stepped forward, ready to trust in the unseen and let faith guide me through whatever would come next.

CHAPTER 6

Bridging Ideals and Realities

THE DAY AFTER THANKSGIVING, WHILE MOST PEOPLE WERE still enjoying leftovers and reflecting on the holiday, I received a call that would shape the next chapter of my life. It wasn't an offer for a new role, but rather an invitation—a request to join the presidential transition team, the group responsible for preparing the incoming administration to take the reins of government on January 20.

The transition between administrations is a critical time, often described as a handoff of immense power, but what it truly requires is a delicate balance of strategy, foresight, and the ability to manage expectations in the face of uncertainty. I had seen transitions from the outside, but this time I would be part of the process, helping to lay the foundation for the work ahead.

What's fascinating about transitions is that they exist in the space between two worlds: the campaign, where the promises are made, and the governance, where those promises are tested against reality. How do you bridge that chasm? How do you ensure that the ideals you've fought for on the trail survive the harsh realities of leading a divided nation? Even as I joined the team, there were no guarantees. The transition itself didn't promise a permanent role in the administration. I found myself in a place of deep reflection, contemplating the uncertainty of my next steps. After months of nonstop work, I faced the question of whether I should continue down this unpredictable path or return to something more stable.

But isn't that the nature of crossroads? They force us to choose between the comfort of what we know and the potential of what we cannot yet see.

During that time, as I navigated the transition into the administration, my wife and I were also facing a transition of our own—a deeply personal one that tested our faith in ways we didn't anticipate. Brittany and I had been married for nearly a decade and had long hoped for children, but the journey had been anything but smooth. When doctors told us that Brittany had large fibroids—ones that could potentially cause serious complications during pregnancy if left untreated—we knew we were at a crossroads. We could either move forward in faith and pursue the surgical procedure to remove the fibroids her doctors recommended, trusting that it would help pave the way for the future we had long prayed for. Or we could allow fear to take hold—leaving the fibroids untreated and hoping for the best, even as the risks loomed over us.

Here's what I've learned about faith and fear: Faith is tied to action, while fear often disguises itself as inaction. Sometimes hope without action isn't hope at all—it's fear wrapped in the illusion of safety.

We chose faith.

That December, just a month after the election was called, as I began my work on the presidential transition team, Brittany prepared for her surgery at NYU Langone Hospital. The morning of the procedure was bitterly cold, with blizzardlike condi-

> *Hope without action isn't hope at all—it's fear wrapped in the illusion of safety.*

tions making it nearly impossible to drive. We left our car behind, walking hand in hand through the snowy streets of East Harlem to catch the subway downtown. The biting wind stung our faces, but I held on to one thought: We were moving forward. No matter how uncertain the path seemed, we were moving forward in faith.

After kissing her goodbye and watching her disappear behind the operating room doors, I made my way to the waiting room. There, with my laptop in hand, I worked on outlining my vision for what DEI could and should look like if I were ever given the opportunity to join the White House staff. The storm outside mirrored the storm inside me—a mixture of hope, fear, and determination. But as I typed, I reminded myself of a lesson I had learned time and time again: Faith doesn't always erase fear, but it does give you the courage to keep going.

The surgery was successful, and Brittany made a healthy recovery. But the greatest miracle of all came months later—Brittany was pregnant. Against all odds, after years of waiting and praying, we were expecting twins. The timing felt divine, a reminder that God's plans often exceed our own.

Amid the uncertainty of the transition period, other enticing opportunities began to emerge. A role at the Obama Foundation offered a chance to contribute to an organization carrying forward the legacy of a president I deeply admired. There was even the prospect of reconnecting with my passion for sports leadership through the NFL. Each option seemed ideal on the surface—a return to stability, prestige, and alignment with my values.

However, something held me back. A quiet nudge reminded me that my journey wasn't over yet. These weren't rejections but redirections—gentle reminders to trust in the unseen and wait for what was truly meant for me. Sometimes the hardest thing to do is to hold still, to resist the pull of the obvious next step and remain open to the unknown.

As I reflected on these possibilities, one moment stood out—a revelation I couldn't ignore. Months earlier, the friend I had once provided advice and insight to during his candidacy for the NFL's first-ever Chief Diversity and Inclusion Officer made history by becoming the first Black NFL team president. His groundbreaking achievement came just as the league hired its inaugural Chief Diversity and Inclusion Officer—a role I had once envisioned for myself.

> *Sometimes the hardest thing to do is to hold still, to resist the pull of the obvious next step and remain open to the unknown.*

The timing felt divinely orchestrated. His journey into history served as a reminder that the seeds we plant often bear fruit in ways we least expect. As he stepped into his historic role, I paused to consider the possibility of working together, but, much like the other opportunities, I felt a nudge to wait. To trust. To believe that something greater was on the horizon.

As I stood at this crossroads, I realized that the journey wasn't just about finding the next step; it was about trusting that the right step would find me.

A Historic Call: Redefining Possibilities

In life, there are moments when the waiting, the trusting, and the quiet nudges all converge into something extraordinary. After months of navigating uncertainty and wrestling with questions about my next steps, I had reached a place of surrender—a willingness to let the right opportunity find me. And then, it did.

That evening, Brittany and I had planned a rare moment of

peace. A much-needed date night at 1 Hotel Brooklyn Bridge was our chance to reconnect and reflect after the whirlwind of the campaign season. As we sat overlooking the skyline, the city lights dancing across the water, I felt an unshakable sense of gratitude—not just for where we were, but for how far we had come. And then, my phone buzzed.

At first, I hesitated to answer. This night was supposed to be about stepping away from the noise of the world, but something in me said to pick up. On the other end was the Biden campaign manager. She had recently been appointed to a senior role in the Biden-Harris administration, and the tone of her voice carried both urgency and excitement.

"President-elect Biden has a vision for this administration," she began. "A vision where diversity, equity, and inclusion aren't just talking points—they're core values that are embedded in the very foundation of how we govern. In all the years of presidential administrations, there has never been a dedicated role focused solely on championing diversity, equity, and inclusion within the White House itself. This is a gap we are determined to fill."

I could feel the weight of her words settling in. This wasn't just about being asked to join the administration; this was something bigger.

Then came the proposition that would forever change my life.

"We want to translate the work you did on the campaign into this new role—an unprecedented position." I was being asked to consider becoming the White House's first-ever Chief Diversity and Inclusion Officer.

For a moment, time seemed to stand still.

I glanced over at Brittany, who must have sensed the gravity of the conversation. Her eyes widened as I mouthed the words: *They want me to lead diversity and inclusion for the White House.* I could feel the enormity of the moment settle over us.

Could this really be happening? After years of advocating for diversity and inclusion in the NFL, on the campaign, and in countless other spaces, I was being asked to shape a groundbreaking role at the highest levels of government. This wasn't just another career opportunity—it was a calling.

Moments like these force you to confront everything you thought you knew about yourself—your faith, your courage, and your readiness to step into the unknown. Saying yes wasn't about ambition or even opportunity—it was about purpose. It was about trusting that all the closed doors, the delays, and the doubts had been preparing me for this exact moment, and so I said yes.

"Yes," I said, my voice steady even as my heart raced. "I'm ready." As I hung up the phone, a wave of emotions rushed over me—gratitude, excitement, and yes, a healthy dose of fear, but isn't that the nature of faith? To walk into the unknown, not because you're fearless but because you trust that what lies ahead is bigger than your fears.

Faith has a way of calling us into the unexpected, and yet, those are often the places we are meant to make the most impact. This was one of those moments—a convergence of my past experiences and my passion for DEI, and a chance to contribute to meaningful change at the highest level.

In the days that followed, the enormity of what I had just agreed to began to sink in. This wasn't just about taking on a new role; it was about building something entirely new from the ground up.

Without an existing job description or blueprint to follow, I had the unique opportunity to shape the role of Chief Diversity and Inclusion Officer for the White House. Collaborating with senior leaders, I began to outline how this position could influence policies, embed DEI principles into the administration's DNA, and set a precedent for future governments.

This wasn't just about representation—it was about reshaping how government serves the people. It was about ensuring that the decisions made at the highest levels of power reflected the diversity and lived experiences of the nation.

I knew it wouldn't be easy. Leadership at this level rarely is. The work ahead would require not only vision and strategy but also resilience in the face of inevitable challenges.

I couldn't help but reflect on the journey that had brought me here. The road had been anything but straightforward, filled with unexpected turns, setbacks, and moments of doubt. Yet, in hindsight, every step had been necessary—each one shaping me, refining me, and preparing me for what was to come. This chapter of my life wasn't just about creating change; it was about helping to bridge the gap between the ideals we preach and the realities we live. It was about turning promises into progress and ensuring that the principles of equity and inclusion didn't just remain words on a page but became the foundation of how we lead.

The real work was only just beginning. As I prepared to walk into history, I knew the next chapter of this journey would require everything I had—and more.

CHAPTER 7

The Wake-Up Call

IT WAS INAUGURATION DAY, JANUARY 20, 2021—A DAY THAT held the weight of history and the promise of something new. The air was brisk, with the sun cutting through the cold, as if to remind us that even after the darkest days, light always finds a way. Yet, lingering beneath the celebratory tone was the undeniable weight of uncertainty—a reminder of how fragile our democracy had felt just two weeks prior.

The memory of January 6, 2021, was fresh—a day when chaos and violence erupted at the Capitol, threatening the foundation of our democracy. But now, standing at the threshold of a new administration, the world was watching. This moment wasn't just about celebration; it was about reckoning. How do you rebuild trust when it has been so deeply fractured? How do you bridge the gap between the ideals we proclaim and the realities we confront?

For me, the tension of the day mirrored the tension within myself. I stood on the brink of a role that had never existed before, feeling both excitement and anxiety. Faith told me I was where I was meant to be; fear whispered reminders of the unknown challenges ahead. Faith and fear, walking hand in hand, each asking the same question: Are you ready?

At what point do we collect enough evidence of God's faithfulness to make our doubts fade? When is it enough? Or do those doubts return every time we stand at the brink of something new, something bigger than ourselves?

Watching Joe Biden and Kamala Harris take their oaths of office was a moment I'll never forget. The symbolism of it all was profound. I thought back to a conversation I'd had with President Biden a year earlier, on New Year's Day, where we talked about how we would reach this very day—with a team that looked like America. And here we were, witnessing the first woman, the first Black woman, the first Asian American, and the first daughter of immigrants being sworn in as vice president of the United States. It was a moment over two centuries in the making—powerful, overdue, and deeply moving.

But as powerful as that moment was, it raised deeper questions: What does it say about our country that it took more than two centuries to arrive at this moment? Does progress always come in these sudden bursts, or is it too gradual to see in real time? How do we measure the distance between where we've been and where we still need to go? These questions have no easy answers, but they are essential to understanding the work that lies ahead—not just in one administration but in the continuous arc of history.

The inauguration was unlike any in history. While it marked a new chapter, it also underscored the uncertainty of the moment. The COVID-19 pandemic had rewritten the rules of everything, including how we celebrated this milestone. Hundreds of political appointees, myself included, were sworn in virtually—a ceremony conducted from living rooms and home offices across the country. It was a reminder that even in times of disruption, the work of governance must continue. President Biden's words echoed through the digital divide, emphasizing public service as a privilege and calling for unity, integrity, and transparency. Yet, unity remains one of the most challenging ideals to achieve, especially in a nation so deeply divided. Transparency, too, is only as strong as the trust that supports it. And trust—fragile as it is—must be rebuilt piece by piece, decision by decision.

These themes—unity, transparency, and trust—are not bound to one leader or one moment. They are the foundation of any functioning democracy, yet they must be actively nurtured to endure. As history has shown, leadership changes, priorities shift, and political tides ebb and flow. The deeper work of building trust and fostering inclusion transcends any administration. It is the thread that connects the past, present, and future of our democracy.

Looking ahead, the questions lingered: What happens when the ideals of unity and inclusion are tested by new leadership? How do we ensure that the progress made doesn't unravel with the inevitable shifts of power? The answers, I realized, lie not in the headlines of any one presidency but in the collective commitment of those who believe in a more inclusive and equitable future.

By the end of that historic day, I was officially the Special Assistant to the President and Chief Diversity and Inclusion Officer. Yet, even as I embraced the opportunity to shape a new cultural blueprint, I couldn't ignore the unique challenges ahead. The paradox was clear: I was working for the White House, but not *in* the White House. The pandemic had transformed how governance operated, thrusting us into a remote world where the physical distance mirrored the social and political divides we were tasked with addressing.

The challenges of my role weren't just logistical; they were structural. The federal government, like the nation it serves, is a vast and intricate ecosystem. It isn't a singular, unified entity but a mosaic of offices, agencies, political appointees, and career civil servants, each with its own priorities, pressures, and pace. Navigating this web required more than just authority—it demanded trust, understanding, and a willingness to meet people where they were.

I quickly learned that building trust in this environment meant understanding the distinct roles within the system. Political appointees like myself come and go with the administration, tasked with executing the president's agenda, but career civil servants are the backbone, the thread of continuity between administrations, carrying the institutional knowledge of how things truly get done. Bridging the gap between these groups wasn't just a priority; it was essential for realizing any progress.

> *Leadership, like life, often delivers its own wake-up calls.*

During the foundational period of my role in the White House—when trust was still being built meeting by meeting, and every new challenge tested our adaptability—I found myself navigating both the structural realities of government and the personal toll leadership often demands. But leadership, like life, often delivers its own wake-up calls—moments that force you to confront what truly matters beyond the day-to-day responsibilities. While I was laying the groundwork for progress in the administration, life was preparing me for a different kind of wake-up call—one that couldn't be solved in a briefing or meeting room.

Life doesn't always wait for you to finish laying the foundation. By May 1, 2022, during my second year in the White House, the focus of my attention shifted dramatically when Brittany called out to me from upstairs at home.

"I think my water just broke," she said, her voice steady but laced with concern.

It was the end of White House Correspondents' Dinner weekend events, and just days earlier, we'd had a false alarm. We were cautious but decided to head to the hospital for peace of mind.

Brittany was thirty-one weeks pregnant, inching toward the critical thirty-two-week milestone that doctors had emphasized. They admitted her for observation, confirming that only one of the amniotic sacs had partially ruptured. The goal was to keep her pregnant for as long as possible, giving our babies more time to grow.

That night, I stayed by her side in the hospital, holding her hand and praying silently that everything would be okay. The hours passed, and with no signs of labor or pain, the doctors reassured us that things were stable. I stayed overnight, sleeping on the small, uncomfortable hospital recliner next to her bed, waking up intermittently to check on her or speak with the night nurses.

The next day, May 2, I remained by her side, grateful for her strength and resilience. We spent the day talking, reflecting on how far we had come in this pregnancy. As evening fell, Brittany, ever calm and reassuring, insisted that I go home to gather a few essentials we had left behind when we rushed to the hospital. "I'm fine," she said, placing her hand on mine. "Just come back first thing in the morning. We'll call you if anything changes." I hesitated, not wanting to leave her. But after the doctors reiterated that she was stable and in good hands, I finally agreed. I left close to midnight, kissed her goodbye, and promised to return first thing in the morning.

I got home, quickly gathered the essentials Brittany had asked for, and crawled into bed just after 1 a.m., exhausted but relieved that she was okay. I set my alarm for early morning, planning to be back at the hospital before sunrise. As I drifted off to sleep, I whispered a silent prayer of gratitude, never imagining what was about to unfold.

Barely an hour later, my phone rang.

I shot up in bed, heart racing, as I grabbed the phone. The voice on the other end was frantic. "Mr. Leach, you need to get to the hospital immediately," the nurse said. "One of the umbilical cords has prolapsed, and we need to act quickly to save the baby. We only have minutes."

My heart dropped, and the grogginess of sleep was instantly replaced by panic. I bolted out of bed, threw on clothes, and sprinted to the car. My hands gripped the steering wheel tightly, my breath heavy as I sped through the empty streets of DC. The city, usually alive with noise, felt eerily silent, as if the world itself was holding its breath along with me.

Fear clawed at the edges of my mind. The words "minutes to act" echoed in my head like a siren. I prayed aloud, over and over: "God, please. Please protect them. Please protect Brittany. Please." Tears blurred my vision, but I couldn't afford to slow down. I pushed the car harder, faster, desperate to reach her in time.

When I arrived at the hospital, I burst past security, breathless and frantic, demanding answers. The doctor approached me, her tone steady but serious, as she explained what had happened. "We identified the prolapsed cord during a routine check. There was no time to wait. We had to perform the emergency C-section within minutes to prevent oxygen deprivation and serious complications." From the moment they detected the complication to the time they delivered the twins, only eight minutes had passed. Eight minutes. God's number for new beginnings.

Prolapsed umbilical cords are rare, occurring in less than 1 percent of births, but when they do happen, they present an extreme emergency. The cord slips into the birth canal ahead of the baby, cutting off the baby's oxygen supply. Without immediate intervention, the consequences can be fatal. I later learned this from the doctor when I arrived, and the weight of it was overwhelming. Black maternal health disparities are real. Even with all the medical advances of recent decades, Black women in the United States remain disproportionately at risk of pregnancy complications and adverse outcomes. Knowing this and that they had only minutes to act—and did—was a sobering reminder of how fragile this moment was, intensifying my prayers for my wife and our daughters.

As I absorbed what she told me, one thought cut through everything: Black maternal health is real. The statistics and risks we had known all along were no longer abstract—they were our reality. But here we were, by God's grace, on the other side of it. The twins had made it, and Brittany, though exhausted and still recovering, was safe.

I felt a wave of emotions: relief that they had acted quickly, guilt for not being by Brittany's side when it happened, and overwhelming gratitude that our babies were here. As if sensing my distress, the doctor gently explained that even if I had been at the hospital, I wouldn't have been allowed in the operating room. The urgency of the situation had required putting Brittany to sleep immediately, leaving no time for anything else. Their policy was clear in cases like this, and while it didn't erase my frustration, it did give me a measure of understanding. "Your daughters are in the NICU," the nurse continued. "They're early, but they're strong."

I insisted on seeing them immediately.

As I stepped into the NICU and saw their tiny, fragile bodies hooked up to monitors and incubators, my knees nearly buckled from the weight of it all. Lela and Nia, eight weeks early but full of fight. I leaned over their incubators, watching their chests rise and fall, and whispered, "You made it. You're here." Tears streamed down my face as I thanked God for carrying us through.

I knew what I needed to do next. I needed to be the first voice Brittany heard when she woke up. I needed her to know that she had done it—that she had carried them safely to this point and that she was covered in God's grace.

I sat beside her bed, holding her hand as she began to stir. "Britt," I whispered, my voice soft but steady. "The girls are here. They're okay. You did it. God has us covered." Her eyes filled with tears, and for a moment, the chaos faded. All that mattered was that we were together and our daughters were alive.

What do you do when the miracle you've been waiting for arrives sooner than you're expecting it to? You lean into the faith that has carried you this far, trusting that God's timing—no matter how unexpected—is always perfect.

But the days and weeks that followed reminded me that miracles don't always come without challenges. We spent more than seven consecutive weeks in the NICU at Georgetown University Hospital, working hand in hand with the medical team to help Lela and Nia grow strong enough to come home with us. Those weeks were some of the most strenuous and emotionally exhausting of my life. The constant sound of monitors beeping, the sterile smell of hospital corridors, and the emotional rollercoaster of watching our daughters fight for every ounce of strength—it tested us in ways we had never imagined.

During this time, I took paternity leave from the White House. My role, my responsibilities, the demands of the administration— all of it took a back seat as I prioritized my family. But even then, the outside world found its way in. There were moments when senior leaders from the White House reached out with urgent or pressing matters. And while I answered a few of those calls, I often found myself in deep internal conflict. Sitting next to my daughters in the NICU, watching them fight for their lives, it was hard to reconcile how any issue in the office could feel more important than this. The calls served as a reminder of the tension that often exists in leadership—between duty and personal life, between responsibility and what truly matters.

By the time we brought Lela and Nia home eight weeks later, I was profoundly changed. The experience had stripped away any illusion of control and left me with a deeper understanding of surrender, resilience, and faith.

As I prepared to return to the White House, I knew I wasn't the same person who had walked through its doors during the first year of the administration. I was stronger, more grounded, and more certain than ever that faith wasn't just a belief—it was the bridge that carried me through the unexpected. But with that new-found clarity came a sharper understanding of the mission before me: I wasn't returning to simply resume the work—I was returning to redefine it, with a focus on building something that could last beyond the daily pressures of the administration.

Returning to the White House with a renewed sense of purpose, I understood that defining my role wouldn't be a one-time task—it was an evolving process. I held tightly to advice I had read in *The One Thing* by Gary Keller and Jay Papasan: "Most people get lost trying to do too much and, in the end, accomplish too little." That wisdom resonated deeply. Isn't that the challenge for all of us? We get so caught up in trying to solve every problem, to be everything to everyone, that we forget to focus on what truly matters. For me, that meant narrowing my focus. The scope of diversity, equity, and inclusion work is vast, and the expectations placed on my shoulders often felt insurmountable.

People from across the country were reaching out, and naturally assumed that, as the Chief Diversity and Inclusion Officer, I was responsible for DEI across the entire federal government—the largest employer in the nation, with nearly three million employees at the time.

Here's the reality: No single person could shoulder that responsibility. My focus had to be clear and intentional. My mission wasn't to solve every DEI issue in government; it was to create a model of inclusion at the center of power—the White House. If we could build a culture of equity and inclusion within the most visible office in the land, the ripple effects would extend outward, influencing agencies and departments across the government.

Clarity Amid Complexity

In those early months, much of my work centered on alignment—meeting with senior leaders in the Chief of Staff's office and other key departments to clarify my role and responsibilities. These conversations were critical in defining what success would look like, even when success itself was a moving target. Leadership in a pioneering role is often about navigating ambiguity, and this was no exception.

Success wasn't about grand gestures; it was about setting the foundation for systemic change. I began with a simple but ambitious goal: to foster a workplace culture that reflected the nation's diversity while empowering every team member to feel seen, heard, and valued, equipped to contribute. That culture couldn't be mandated; it had to be built through intention, consistency, and action.

A pivotal moment in shaping this culture came during our first all-staff meeting. It was an opportunity to set the tone, to unite a scattered workforce around a shared vision. This wasn't just about logistics; it was about leadership in its truest form—casting a vision that people could rally around.

Instead of diving into the technicalities of DEI initiatives, I focused on themes that transcended the moment: learning and development, connection and community, trust and collaboration. These were the pillars I believed could hold us together, even in the face of distance and division. As I addressed the team, I spoke not just of what we aimed to accomplish but why it mattered, laying out the mission and vision for DEI in the White House, framing it in a way that not only connected to their work but to their sense of purpose.

The first focus? **Learning and Development**. "We should never stop learning because life never stops teaching," I reminded them. I asked each person to reflect on that truth: How many times have we missed the lesson because we thought we already knew the answer? I wanted them to see this not as an obligation but as an opportunity for growth, for self-reflection, for becoming better versions of ourselves so we could become better stewards of the administration's mission.

Next, I spoke about the second focus: **Connection and Community**. "Everyone communicates, but few connect," I said, paraphrasing a thought that has always stayed with me from John C. Maxwell. How often do we move through life speaking without listening, engaging without truly seeing each other? Creating spaces for connection was vital, especially in the midst of physical separation. Our work wasn't just about policy or process; it was about people. I urged them to see one another—not just as colleagues but as contributors to something bigger than any one of us.

Finally, I turned to the third focus: **Trust and Collaboration**. "Trust is the foundation upon which everything rests," I said. "And transparency breeds trust." Without it, collaboration would be a hollow endeavor. I emphasized that our ability to drive progress was inseparable from our ability to trust one another—to share openly, to give without expectation, to collaborate knowing that each person's contribution was necessary to achieving our collective goals.

"This work, to champion DEI," I continued, "will take all of us, not just some of us. This isn't a passive effort; it's an active responsibility. We will do it one day at a time, one person at a time."

The message resonated, not because it offered a detailed road map but because it reminded us of our shared purpose. Almost immediately after I finished speaking, messages began coming in—notes of appreciation, encouragement, and offers of support from colleagues across the administration. Even the Chief of Staff at the time, Ron Klain, reached out directly, reinforcing his commitment and letting me know that if I ever needed anything, his door was open. That's the thing about leadership—it's not always about providing answers; sometimes it's about inspiring others to find their own.

The work that followed was both rewarding and relentless. Together with senior leaders, I began crafting the frameworks that would guide our DEI efforts—not just for this administration but for those to come. This meant embedding equity into hiring practices, launching the first-ever paid White House internship program, and ensuring that our team reflected the nation's diversity in a way that wasn't just symbolic but meaningful.

Progress wasn't always easy to measure, especially in a role that required both strategic vision and operational precision, but I held on to a simple truth: Real change doesn't happen in a vacuum. It requires relationships, collaboration, and a willingness to confront uncomfortable truths.

As I worked to cultivate this change, I often reflected on a concept that has shaped my approach to leadership: the power of culture. Michael D. Watkins, in his book *The First 90 Days*, defines culture as "a set of consistent patterns people follow for communicating, thinking, and acting, all grounded in their shared assumptions and values." It's a simple yet profound truth, one that extends beyond organizations to communities, nations, and even movements. Culture isn't just what we say we value—it's what we demonstrate through our actions, our decisions, and our everyday interactions.

The culture of any institution—whether it's the White House, a company, or a country—is shaped not only by its leaders but by the collective actions of its people. When it comes to the culture of a nation as complex and diverse as the United States, those actions must be guided by principles that reflect our shared humanity. That's why DEI isn't just a policy initiative or a set of programs; it's a lens through which we examine how we communicate, think, and act toward one another. It's about fostering a culture where every individual feels seen, valued, and empowered to contribute.

This perspective gave me clarity amid complexity. I realized that while the policies we implemented and the milestones we achieved were important, the true measure of success lay in the culture we were building. Were we creating an environment where diverse voices were not just included but amplified? Were we embedding equity into the fabric of our decisions in a way that could withstand the shifts and cycles of political power?

As time progressed, so did our efforts. During my tenure in the first year of the administration, President Biden signed Executive Order 14035, advancing diversity, equity, inclusion, and accessibility (DEIA) across the federal government. The Government-Wide Strategic Plan to Advance DEIA in the Federal Workforce was released soon after, embedding equity principles not just in rhetoric but in the operational framework of federal agencies.

One of the most significant milestones for the administration was launching the first-ever paid White House internship program. For years, the lack of compensation for interns had created barriers to entry, especially for first-generation college students, applicants from communities of color, and those from low-income backgrounds. This program wasn't just a policy shift; it was a statement about the kind of administration we wanted to be—one that opened doors and leveled the playing field.

By 2023, we reached a historic milestone: Nearly half of the White House staff who served came from racially and ethnically diverse communities—establishing us as the most diverse White House staff in US history. This wasn't about quotas or numbers; it was about building a culture where people could see themselves reflected in the spaces where decisions were made.

Here's the thing about progress: It's often misunderstood. The visible milestones are easy to celebrate, but the true work happens in the unseen moments. It's in the quiet persistence, the willingness to confront uncomfortable truths, and the determination to build something lasting, even when applause fades.

Yet, even as we moved forward, I was keenly aware of the broader political landscape. History has shown that the priorities of one administration can be dismantled by the next, but I believed, and still believe, that the principles of DEI and inclusive leadership—valuing every voice, creating space for every story—are not tied to any one leader or party. They are tied to the fabric of our democracy and the promise of equity for all.

It's this recognition that makes DEI work so urgent and so necessary. As the nation grows more diverse each year, the culture we cultivate—through leadership, through governance, through our shared values—becomes even more essential. This isn't just about making room for diversity; it's about ensuring that our institutions, our workplaces, and our communities reflect the lived experiences of the people they serve.

Why is this so important? Because true equity goes beyond representation—it's about recognizing that not everyone starts from the same place and meeting people where they are. Think about a track-and-field race. Every runner is competing in the same four-hundred-meter sprint, but not everyone starts at the same place. Some runners begin at the official starting line, equipped with the best gear and years of professional coaching. Others are forced to start ten steps behind—because their families were denied opportunities to accumulate wealth, education, or social capital. Some wear weights around their ankles, carrying the burdens of systemic barriers that others never had to consider. The race is the same distance for all, but the starting points are not.

Now, imagine standing at the finish line and calling it a fair race simply because everyone ran four hundred meters. Would that be justice? Would that reflect the reality of effort and opportunity? Or would it ignore the very real disadvantages that shaped the outcome before the race even began?

Equity is about removing those weights, closing those gaps, and ensuring that no one is held back by circumstances beyond their control. It's not about unfair advantages—it's about acknowledging that fairness isn't just about the race itself, but about the conditions under which people enter it. Equality says we all get the same; equity says we all get what we need. By addressing these unique starting points, we create pathways for everyone to succeed. It's about understanding that while we all have different starting points, the progress we make together must be equitable for it to be meaningful.

=====

Leadership is rarely a solo endeavor. That truth became even clearer to me in the weeks following the inauguration when a significant opportunity emerged. A senior leader in the White House Cabinet Affairs Office, and a trusted colleague from my days on the campaign, reached out. He asked me to deliver a high-level briefing on DEI to the president's Cabinet members. This was no small task. Each Cabinet member was in the process of building out their leadership teams, and it was crucial that diversity, equity, and inclusion were at the forefront of those decisions.

It was an opportunity not just to inform but to influence—to set the tone for how DEI principles would permeate the administration's work. I knew the stakes were high; the decisions made in that room could ripple across the federal government, shaping how these leaders approached DEI, and would set a precedent for the rest of their agencies and, ultimately, for the country. Whether it was rallying staff in a remote setting or briefing Cabinet members on DEI priorities, each moment revealed how essential collaboration is in achieving progress.

In leadership, there's a choice we all face—whether to see moments like this as a competition for attention or as an opportunity for collaboration. The easy path would have been to monopolize the briefing, to claim the entirety of the platform for myself. But what I knew, and what I had learned in my journey so far, was that real progress isn't made by one person alone. It takes a collective effort, a unifying of voices, experiences, and expertise.

Collaboration was at the heart of my approach. I invited leaders from the Presidential Personnel Office (PPO) and the Office of Personnel Management (OPM) to join me in the briefing. Together, we emphasized that DEI wasn't just a responsibility—it was a value, one that required buy-in at every level of leadership. Their insights were instrumental in helping Cabinet members see DEI not as a standalone initiative but as a guiding principle embedded in their decision-making.

As I addressed the Cabinet, I made one point clear: "We must move from compliance to commitment." Diversity and inclusion couldn't be seen as check-the-box exercises; they had to be woven into the fabric of decision-making. From hiring practices to policy implementation, every choice carried the potential to either deepen or disrupt the work of equity.

The questions that followed weren't just logistical; they were reflective. Leaders wanted to know how to identify blind spots, how to foster inclusive cultures within their departments, and how to balance competing priorities without losing sight of equity. Their engagement was a reminder that even at the highest levels, leadership is a process of learning and unlearning, of humility and action.

There's a lesson here that transcends my role or this specific moment: Leadership isn't about holding on to power. It's about distributing it wisely, about understanding that the more you uplift others, the stronger your collective efforts become. This was a message I wanted to convey to the Cabinet as well—that DEI wasn't the responsibility of any one individual or office. It had to be woven into the fabric of every agency, championed by every leader, and supported by teams that believed in the power of inclusion.

Not every pivotal moment was as high stakes as the Cabinet briefing, but each one mattered in its own way. Whether it was hosting a fireside chat with Dr. Anthony Fauci for staff across the administration or engaging with junior staff alongside singer-songwriter and actress Olivia Rodrigo during a short visit to the White House, these moments reinforced the power of connection.

I realized that the work of DEI wasn't confined to policy or strategy—it was also about creating spaces where people felt seen and valued. Olivia's visit, for instance, wasn't just a morale booster for our team; it was a reminder that representation matters. Her presence inspired junior staff to see themselves as part of a larger story, one where their contributions were essential to the administration's success.

Progress isn't always linear, and it's rarely flashy.

Dr. Fauci's fireside chat offered a different kind of reflection. As he prepared to step down from public service, he spoke about the human side of leadership—the need for empathy, resilience, and the courage to lead through uncertainty. His words stayed with me, a reminder that leadership isn't just about what you do; it's about how you make people feel.

These moments—big and small—helped build a culture of trust, collaboration, and shared purpose. They reminded me that progress isn't always linear, and it's rarely flashy. It's the cumulative effect of choices made with intention.

Progress and Pressure

For every visible victory, there were unseen struggles—battles fought behind closed doors, meetings where hard truths were shared, and moments of doubt that crept in after long days of work. The reality of being the first-ever meant navigating uncharted waters, often without a clear road map or sufficient resources. The pressure felt insurmountable at times, as the expectations placed on my shoulders clashed with the limitations of my role. In those moments, I leaned on my faith and the lessons I'd learned along the way. Leadership, I reminded myself, isn't about perfection; it's about progression.

The work wasn't just about getting results; it was about sustaining progress. It required navigating the politics of the building and ensuring that my efforts weren't overshadowed by the relentless pace of the administration's broader priorities. Make no mistake, the White House is a fast-moving machine. The daily urgency to deliver often ran counter to the longer-term, more structural goals that DEI demanded.

Over time, I found myself grappling with an unsettling reality: While I had influence, I wasn't positioned at the same level as some of my colleagues. The commissioned officer designation in my title

was Special Assistant to the President—significant, no doubt—
but it wasn't quite at the level of Deputy Assistant or Assistant to
the President, which are positioned higher and garner much more
influence and authority. The distinction may sound subtle, but in
the corridors of the White House, such distinctions weren't merely
symbolic; they shaped not only the perception of influence but
also the ability to drive change. I faced a question that many leaders encounter: Was I being given enough tools to truly succeed in
this role? Could I bring about the systemic changes necessary when
my position didn't always afford me the same level of influence
as those around me? These questions lingered, but I had come to
realize something important: True leadership isn't about titles, it's
about impact. It's about using whatever platform you have—no
matter how big or small—to make a difference.

Still, the weight of the work remained. There were moments
when I began to notice cracks in the foundation, even in the most
well-intentioned spaces. Inclusion could fall short—not out of
malice but from the inertia of long-standing systems.

In the months ahead, I would face moments that tested everything I thought I knew about leadership, inclusion, and the
culture we were building. One such moment came during the
White House Black History Month reception in 2023. While the
reception was undeniably a celebration of progress, my personal
experience that day revealed an uncomfortable truth: how far we
still had to go in ensuring that inclusion was a lived reality for
everyone—especially for those advocating for those very values every single day.

It was a turning point, one that shattered assumptions and exposed the shadows of exclusion that lingered—even in spaces meant
to embody equity and inclusion. As those shadows stretched, they
demanded answers I wasn't sure anyone was ready to confront, not
even me.

That's the nature of this work—it's never a straight line toward resolution. The pursuit of equity and inclusion will always be tested by resistance, inertia, and discomfort. Yet, we push forward, knowing that every gain is a battle and every setback a reminder that progress demands persistence, not perfection.

What I had learned—both from the personal wake-up call of my daughters' birth and my professional challenges within the White House—was that change isn't guaranteed, but it is possible. It's built through intention, consistency, and the collective efforts of those who refuse to give up. The tension between faith and fear never fully disappears, but that tension, I realized, is what makes progress possible.

This work doesn't rely on proximity to power. Even as political tides shift and different ideologies come into play, the seeds you plant today can still inspire future action. Real progress lives beyond policy; it's found in the lasting imprint you leave on people's hearts and minds—their sense of what's possible, what engagement can look like, and how they, too, can drive change personally, professionally, and civically.

As I stepped into what would become one of the most challenging moments of my time in the White House, I carried this knowledge with me: The work isn't about immediate victories—it's about making sure the work outlasts any single moment and continues long after we're gone.

As I would soon discover, the hardest battles aren't always fought against outside forces. Sometimes, the greatest challenges show up within the spaces we trust the most—reminding us that even safe havens can harbor unseen trials, and that only faith and resilience can help us become stronger on the other side.

CHAPTER 8

Shadows of Exclusion

SOME LESSONS DON'T ARRIVE IN MEMOS OR PRESS BRIEFINGS; they arrive at the door—literally. We can spend years championing inclusion, convinced the doorway will stand open for everyone, only to discover that in the very moment meant to celebrate progress, inclusion still comes with an asterisk. As I set off toward the East Room for the 2023 Black History Month reception, I thought I understood those unspoken rules. That night, I learned how invisible—and how personal—they can be.

Before we get there, I want to take you back to a moment that foreshadowed this experience—a moment that took place not in the White House, but in the world of sports, where I had once found myself at a similar crossroads. As I've shared earlier, working for the NFL had been a dream come true. As a young man, I had always aspired to reach the pinnacle of sports management, and here I was, a key member of the NFL Management Council, representing the billionaire owners of the thirty-two NFL teams. My journey was one of ambition, hard work, and a steadfast belief in the ideals of sportsmanship and fair play. But as I quickly learned, ideals often clash with reality, especially when identity, politics, and power come into play.

In 2016, Colin Kaepernick took a knee—not in submission, but in protest—an act that reverberated beyond the football field. As I shared, Kaepernick's decision to kneel during the national anthem was a stand against systemic racism and injustice, a courageous gesture that came with significant personal cost. Reflecting on that moment now, I can't help but see the parallels between his journey and mine, which I'll explain momentarily. Kaepernick, a man of conviction, found himself on the outside looking in, cast aside by the very institution he had given so much to. His protest was a stark reminder that even those with the courage to stand for what's right are not immune to being excluded.

But here's the question that lingers: What happens when the very system you believed in no longer sees you? What do you do when the ideals you fought for overlook you?

Inside the NFL, the conversations about the protests were challenging to navigate. As part of the Management Council, I knew the delicate balance we had to maintain—supporting players' rights to free speech while navigating the league's commercial interests and public image. Yet despite these efforts, Kaepernick became a controversial figure. His future in the NFL hung in the balance,

> *What happens when the very system you believed in no longer sees you?*

and though measures were introduced to support social justice initiatives, the league's response at the time felt incomplete. Kaepernick found himself without a team, his football playing career seemingly in limbo.

For me, Kaepernick's situation was a sobering reminder of how ideals can clash with reality. More deeply, it forced me to confront the unsettling truth that exclusion doesn't discriminate—it can come for anyone, no matter their contributions or status. This hard truth became all too real when I faced my own moment of exclusion—this time, not on a football field, but in the very halls of power I had worked so hard to serve in.

Struggles in the Shadows

The White House is known for hosting a wide array of special receptions throughout the year, events that serve as moments of recognition and celebration for various groups, causes, and cultural observances. These receptions range from honoring championship sports teams to paying tribute to veterans, arts luminaries, and significant historical milestones. They are designed not only as ceremonial gestures but also as opportunities for the president and the administration to build connections with communities, celebrate their contributions, and highlight the nation's diversity. These events serve as a reflection of the administration's priorities and a way to engage with key stakeholders and advocates.

For me, the Black History Month reception was one of the most anticipated events on the calendar. As the first-ever Chief Diversity and Inclusion Officer, and as a Black man, this reception felt personal—a chance to celebrate progress and history while connecting with leaders and activists whose work mirrored my own. As I made my way to the reception, what should have been a moment of pride and celebration turned into something else entirely.

The walk through the corridors of the White House felt different that evening. The grand hallways, lined with portraits of past presidents and historic moments, felt alive with the weight of history. I walked with a sense of purpose, a mixture of pride and anticipation coursing through me. Underneath it all, there was a tension I couldn't quite place. The rhythmic click of my shoes echoed against the marble floors, a subtle reminder that I was part of this administration, a symbol of progress in a house that had witnessed centuries of American history.

I didn't realize I would soon be asking myself this question: How do you prepare for a moment when the space that should welcome you closes its doors instead?

The East Room, the largest room in the White House, awaited me. It was where presidents had greeted world leaders and signed significant legislation, and where countless historic moments had unfolded. The closer I got, the more my heart swelled with the significance of the occasion. This was it. The culmination of a journey that had brought me to this role, to this house. Black History Month—an observance of the struggles and triumphs of Black Americans—was more than just a symbolic gesture for me. It was a celebration of a legacy I was personally tied to.

Yet, I wasn't on the official guest list. Typically, these lists prioritized external guests—leaders from the community, activists, and advocates—followed by Cabinet secretaries and the most senior staff within the White House. Those of us in newly created roles or without the highest commissioned officer titles often fell outside the automatic inclusions. It was a frustrating reality of working in a space that carried centuries of hierarchical tradition, where titles sometimes mattered more than contributions—but that evening, I believed my work, my contributions, and my role as the administration's first-ever Chief Diversity and Inclusion Officer would transcend those constraints.

With every step, I thought about the people who would be inside—the civil rights leaders, the activists, the change-makers. This was a moment to connect, to further the work, to celebrate how far we had come. The East Room, bathed in the soft glow of chandeliers, felt like the perfect setting for this moment of reflection and unity. I could almost hear the hum of voices from the crowd, feel the warmth of the gathering, the shared sense of purpose that had drawn us all here.

As I approached the entrance, I was stopped by two members of the White House operations team—a team I worked with regularly, people I knew by name—who stood in front of me, blocking the entrance. "Your name isn't on the list," one of them said. At first, I smiled, thinking it was a joke, a momentary misunderstanding. But when I asked, "Are you serious right now?" her response cut through the air like a knife. "I don't care what your role is, but you're not getting in—you're not on the list." There was no room for negotiation, no recognition of the countless hours I had worked with this team. Her words hung heavy in the space between us. No laughter, no lighthearted banter—just the cold reality of exclusion.

In that instant, everything shifted. The pride I had felt moments earlier dissolved into confusion, then disbelief. *How could this be happening?* My title, my work, the countless hours spent fighting for inclusion and representation—they seemed to vanish in the face of an unforgiving guest list. I wasn't just being turned away from a room. I was being turned away from the very celebration of the history I was meant to be part of.

A question haunted me: What do you do when the door closes, not because you haven't earned your place, but because someone else decides you don't belong?

I tried reaching out to senior staff members who were already inside, hoping someone could help resolve the situation but my calls went unanswered. My email to the head of the White House Social Office—the office responsible for organizing the event—were ignored. To this day, I have never received a response.

I had spent much of my career fighting for inclusion. But in this moment, I was being asked to accept exclusion. Where was the lesson in that? Where was the faith in that? It's one thing to believe in purpose when doors open, but what about when they close?

As I walked back toward my office in the Eisenhower Executive Office Building (EEOB), frustration and disbelief washed over me. How could this happen? How could I, a senior leader in this administration, be excluded from a reception that was meant to celebrate Black history? It was a stark reminder that, even when progress is being made, exclusion can still rear its head.

Each step away from that door felt heavier than the last. It didn't matter what I had contributed, the work I had done, or what this moment was supposed to mean. I was outside—literally and figuratively. And for the first time in a long time, I wasn't sure what to do next.

In a stroke of providence, I ran into a colleague who was helping with the day-of logistics. He saw me heading toward my office and casually asked, "Aren't you going to the reception?" When I explained what had happened—that the two members of the operations team, whom we both knew well, had refused me entry—his expression shifted. He could see the frustration and disbelief I had been holding in. He immediately insisted on escorting me back to the event, saying, "You belong in that room, and we'll deal with any fallout later."

This colleague, a white man and a member of the LGBTQIA+ community, used his privilege and position to ensure my entry. The juxtaposition of our identities—the fact that I needed the intervention of someone who didn't share my struggles that day to gain access—was not lost on me. It underscored a painful reality: Sometimes it takes the privilege of others to navigate the spaces we should rightfully belong to. And this is where another question emerged: What does it mean when even those fighting for inclusion need someone else's privilege to be included?

By the time my colleague had ensured my entry into the reception, the program had already begun. I stood in the Grand Foyer, which was being used as the overflow room, and remained there for the duration of the event, watching virtually as it unfolded, feeling a mix of frustration, sadness, and resignation. The celebration was happening, but I wasn't truly part of it.

That night, I barely slept. The weight of what had happened pressed on my chest, gnawing at my spirit like a wound that wouldn't close. Questions swirled in my mind, relentless and sharp: *How could this happen? How could a place I had poured my soul into, an administration I had fought for with everything I had, so easily dismiss me?* My role, my value, my very existence in those halls—everything felt called into question.

I lay there in the stillness of the night, staring at the ceiling, thinking back to the countless sacrifices—the sleepless nights, the early mornings, the moments I missed with my family—all to give my best to this administration. I thought about the weight I carried during the campaign, the long hours, the relentless pursuit of a victory we believed could bring real change. And after all of that, after everything I had given of myself, this is what I was left with. I was unseen, unheard, and discarded in the very space where I had once believed I could make a difference.

One question cut deeper than the exclusion itself: What does it mean when the very place you're fighting to make more inclusive leaves you standing outside its doors?

=

Reflecting on my exclusion from the White House reception and my time in the NFL during Kaepernick's protest, I realized that exclusion is a universal experience—one that transcends industries, roles, and levels of achievement. Whether you're an athlete taking a stand or a leader advocating for change, exclusion can find its way in, challenging your sense of purpose and belonging.

The question is: How do we move forward from these moments? How do we choose faith over fear when the world tells us we don't belong?

In the NFL and the White House, I found myself facing the same core issue: the gap between American ideals and American realities. Both institutions, in their own ways, professed to champion inclusion. Yet in both, I experienced moments that made me question how deeply those ideals were embedded in their structures. I realized that in these moments of exclusion, we have a choice. We can give in to the pain and frustration, or we can choose to keep moving forward, to keep pushing for the change we want to see. Kaepernick's decision to kneel wasn't just an act of protest—it was a declaration of faith in the possibility of a better future. My exclusion from the White House event, painful as it was, reminded me that the fight for inclusion is ongoing and that every moment of adversity can be an opportunity to bridge the divide.

How do we reconcile the ideals we fight for with the reality of exclusion we sometimes face? And more important, how do we keep moving forward when the very places we work to change leave us standing on the outside?

People in all spheres of life, regardless of background, race, gender, or position, will face moments that challenge their sense of belonging. When those moments come, it's easy to give in to fear, to wonder if you're in the right place. *But what if, instead, we chose faith?* Faith in our purpose. Faith in the work we've done. Faith that, even when we're excluded, our value remains intact.

This incident at the White House was never resolved or reconciled, but I've found my own sense of closure through faith. I've become more committed than ever to ensuring that my experience of exclusion doesn't have to be experienced by others. In the weeks that followed, I sought the counsel of trusted confidants, both inside and outside the White House. Some had worked in past administrations; others were deeply entrenched in the political orbit. These were people I trusted to give me honest feedback, seasoned individuals who had weathered the highs and lows of political life. I shared the details of what had happened, explaining just how frustrated, disappointed, and—if I'm being honest—hurt I was by the experience. Each of them shared in my frustration. They, too, were appalled and deeply disappointed by the exclusion I had faced in a space where I should have been included, not sidelined. The gravity of their responses made it clear that this was not just a personal affront; it was indicative of a deeper issue within the very place we were all working so hard to transform.

While I never had the opportunity to address this incident directly with President Biden or Vice President Harris, I remain confident that if they had been made aware of it, they would have taken immediate action to ensure it never happened again. That's the kind of leaders they are—committed to equity, fairness, and inclusion—but the delicate and complex nature of working in the White House made navigating such situations uniquely challenging. President Biden's circle was understandably tight and insular, given the magnitude of responsibilities he faced daily. Escalating an issue like this required careful consideration, and I wasn't willing to bypass the established chain of command for a matter that, while deeply personal, felt less urgent compared to the critical issues of the day.

Initially, I shared my frustration with my direct day-to-day reporting line—a deputy director who suggested I reach out to the teams responsible for organizing the event and work with them to prevent similar oversights in the future. While this advice wasn't malicious, it placed the burden of resolution squarely on my shoulders, at a time when I was already carrying the weight of exclusion, a demanding portfolio, and an under-resourced team. It reminded me of how often staff members of color are left to navigate these moments alone, without allies to champion their cause or walk the path of resolution alongside them.

Months later, I took it upon myself to meet with one of the most senior leaders in the White House, someone within the president's chief of staff office, to share what had happened. This individual, unaware of the incident, expressed genuine empathy and assured me she would reach out to others to ensure it didn't happen again. Her response was kind and sincere, but it was also the extent of the resolution I received. The incident, for all its emotional weight, faded into the background of the White House's relentless pace.

The lack of a more definitive resolution stung, but it underscored a truth I had already come to understand: Moments like these require more than internal reflection. They demand allies willing to advocate alongside you and systems robust enough to prevent exclusion in the first place. It reminded me that progress isn't just about policies or individual actions—it's about building structures and relationships that ensure no one has to face these moments alone.

In the end, I found my own sense of closure—not through resolution, but through faith. The experience underscored an enduring truth: Moments of exclusion are not meant to define us but to refine us. They challenge us to stay grounded in our purpose, even when faced with adversity.

This wasn't just about being excluded from a single event. It was about reckoning with the gap that still exists between the ideals we champion and the realities we face. Exclusion can leave scars, but it can also leave questions—questions that, over time, push us toward deeper understanding and clarity about who we are, what we stand for, and why we continue the fight.

As I reflected on the incident, a deeper thought began to crystallize: What does it mean to persist in spaces that challenge your sense of belonging? How do you reconcile the ideals you fight for with the reality of exclusion?

Exclusion has a way of forcing you into introspection. It makes you question not just the systems around you but the beliefs within you. It pushes you to examine the tension between what you hope to achieve and the resistance you face along the way. Truth is often found in tension—the space where discomfort meets discovery, where struggle reveals clarity. In those moments of questioning, you are left with a choice: Do you allow the weight of exclusion to diminish your purpose, or do you allow it to sharpen your resolve?

That's where the real questions emerged—not just about the spaces I occupied but about myself. What was driving me forward? Was it faith in the work, the people, or the possibility of change? Or was I unknowingly running from fear of what might happen if I stopped? What are you running from, and what are you running for?

These questions stayed with me, shaping the path ahead. They weren't just questions of identity or belonging; they became questions of purpose and perseverance. And over time, they led to a moment of clarity— one that reframed not just my work but my understanding of who I am and what I am called to do.

> *Truth is often found in tension.*

CHAPTER 9

A Moment of Clarity

What Are You ~~Running for~~ Running From?

"WOULD YOU EVER RUN FOR OFFICE ONE DAY?"
The question had been asked several times over the years but this time from a well-meaning colleague during a late-night strategy session. I chuckled, deflecting the question as usual, knowing full well that stepping into the political arena felt like stepping into a storm. I had seen enough to know the weight of that decision, and it was a storm I never intended to chase. But how often do we push away the things we fear, only to find that they still chase us down?

My immediate response has usually been laughter, quickly followed by a subtle deflection. The idea seemed almost absurd to me. I couldn't imagine subjecting myself to what I had witnessed while working on Joe Biden's presidential campaign. The relentless pace, the constant scrutiny, the half-truths and exaggerations that target a candidate's family—these were just the surface of the challenges. Navigating the contentious opposition, the deep divisions, and the hateful rhetoric of a campaign was something I believed was best left to those who felt a profound calling or conviction to endure that cyclical lifestyle.

I have never felt that pull.

Have you ever been urged by others to pursue something that didn't resonate with your own sense of purpose or calling? Something you didn't feel equipped or gifted for? How do you respond to such nudges? And perhaps more important, how do you discern whether your response is the right one?

How often do we allow others' expectations to shape our path? And how do we discern the difference between an external call and an internal conviction? These questions have a way of lingering, gnawing at you in quiet moments when the noise of the day fades away. They creep in during the stillness, demanding to be answered. But how does one find the clarity to answer them? For me, the answer has always been rooted in faith.

> *Prayer should be our first response, not our last resort.*

I learned something valuable in my church community about how we, as people of faith, should respond to questions that stir uncertainty, discomfort, or anxiety. We were taught that prayer should be our first response, not our last resort. It's a simple principle, but one that has profound implications. It's about grounding yourself in something larger than the immediate pressures and expectations of the world around you. So, as I often did during my quiet moments, whenever I felt adrift or nudged to gain clarity, I turned to God in prayer.

The rain tapped softly against the window, an almost rhythmic reminder of time passing. I stood by the window, watching droplets race down the glass, feeling the weight of the world outside these walls. The stillness of the room contrasted with the storm in my heart. I knelt by the bed, as I had so many times before, but this time felt different. I needed clarity, not just for the work I was doing, but for the road ahead. I closed my eyes and sought His guidance, letting my worries dissolve into prayer.

As I knelt there, seeking clarity, the questions from recent months weighed heavily on me—the Black History Month reception, the constant demands of the White House, the exhaustion that had been quietly creeping in. What comes next? How do I continue to serve in a space where at times I had felt so unseen? I prayed for clarity, for direction. But as often happens in moments of prayer, my mind began to wander. I found myself reflecting on everything—my time in the White House, my work on the Biden campaign, and the sacrifices I had made along the way. The intensity of the campaign came rushing back.

Working on a presidential campaign is an all-consuming experience. The promises, the fearmongering, the policy pitches, the endless debates—all of it is part of the machinery, and while necessary, it had often felt like an assault on my spirit. You become so focused on that one singular goal—getting your candidate elected—that every other part of your life fades into the background. The stakes are high, the pressure immense. But what happens after that? When the campaign is over, when the world moves on, what remains?

Maybe that was part of the reason I had thrown myself into the work so relentlessly—not just because I believed in the mission, but because it kept me moving. Kept me busy. Kept me from having to stop and face the bigger questions that loomed in the quiet moments. The exhaustion, the pace, the relentless demands—they gave me a reason not to ask what came next. Had I been using ambition as a shield from something God had been

Was I running toward purpose or just running away from uncertainty?

asking me to step into? Was I running toward purpose or just running away from uncertainty?

As I reflected on those intense months, my thoughts drifted back to the question that had been posed to me many times before joining the campaign, during the campaign, and even after: Would God ever call me to run for office? For mayor? For governor? For Congress? For president? It was a question that always caught me off guard, one I had deflected with laughter and a change of subject, but now, in the stillness of my home, I posed the question to God directly.

I wasn't expecting an answer, but as I sat there in prayer, a different question came to mind: What would you run on?

It was a question that went beyond the surface of political ambition. It was a question about purpose. On what foundation would I stand? What would my message be? What campaign slogan would truly resonate with who I am? And before I could even answer, another question emerged: **Am I running *for* something, or am I just running *from* something?**

The question stopped me in my tracks. What would I run on? It's a question that gets to the heart of who you are, what you believe in, and what you're willing to fight for. And deeper still, it asks: What is it that truly defines your purpose? It's easy to imagine running on the slogans of the day, the ideals we've all heard, but do they align with the reality of your convictions?

As I sat with those questions, I found myself reflecting on the cyclical nature of campaigns, particularly the outsize impact of the presidential cycle on all other levels of government—federal, state, and local. Every election cycle, we often hear the familiar refrain of America's founding ideals: liberty and freedom, equality, democracy, justice, the rule of law, opportunity, the American Dream, and civic responsibility.

These principles are the lifeblood of every political campaign, invoked by candidates as they seek to align themselves with the nation's core values and appeal to voters' sense of patriotism and commitment. And yet, with everything I had witnessed—and continued to witness—the thought stayed with me: Why do these ideals often feel so far removed from the realities of those living in this country, the very people who support the candidates espousing them? Isn't it ironic how the promises of these ideals seem to drift farther from reach for those who need them most?

Well, God, I thought, if I were ever to run for office, my campaign would be the one to turn American ideals into American realities. Year after year, I sensed that people, especially communities of color, were growing weary of hearing politicians speak publicly about ideals that felt like hollow echoes when compared to the stark, private realities they faced daily. There, God, I thought, that's what I would run on. Enough talk about ideals—more action focused on the realities of the people, families, and communities I would serve.

Curiosity led me to my laptop. I wanted to see if any political candidate had ever used or trademarked the phrase "Turning American ideals into American realities." I pulled my laptop closer, the glow of the screen illuminating the darkened room. I typed the words slowly at first, not expecting much. I searched and found nothing. No one.

As I scrolled through pages of results, something caught my eye—an article, buried deep in the archives of history. The name Max Beloff stared back at me from the screen, like a whisper from the past. Who was this person, obscurely tucked away on page eight of my Google search results? Was he a candidate? A government official? Intrigued, I clicked on the link, and the words that followed would stop me in my tracks.

"American Ideals vs. American Realities" was a *New York Times* article published on August 29, 1948, written by this Max Beloff.

Beloff, I discovered, was not a politician but a British historian and political thinker. His insights offered a profound outsider's perspective on the American experience. Born in London in 1913, Beloff's intellectual journey led him to become one of the most respected voices in the study of governance and democracy. His career was illustrious, with positions at Oxford University and as the founding principal of the University of Buckingham. What truly drew me in was his 1948 article, where he critically examined the gap between the lofty ideals that America was founded upon—liberty, democracy, equality—and the often harsh realities of its political and social life.

His article resonated deeply with me because it highlighted the very contradictions I, too, was grappling with—the disparities between the values we preach and the actions we take as a nation. Beloff's outsider perspective allowed him to see clearly what many within America could not or would not acknowledge: that the gap between ideals and realities wasn't just a product of individual failures but of systemic contradictions embedded within the fabric of American society.

How is it that an outsider, writing in the 1940s, could see with such clarity what so many of us have struggled to articulate in modern times? It's easy to become desensitized to the disparities around us, but sometimes it takes someone on the outside to shine a light on the uncomfortable truths we'd rather avoid on the inside. Could it be that we've been too close to the problem to see it for what it really is? As I read on, I was struck by how Beloff's observations from 1948 felt eerily similar to what I was witnessing in present-day America. How, I wondered, could his words from decades ago still ring so true today? Had we not made progress since then? Were the ideals touted back then still so vastly different from the realities we live in now? My heart raced as I continued reading.

Some of Beloff's most resonant quotes seemed to echo not just through time but through the very fabric of American society today. "I have been here before," he wrote, as if to suggest that history has a way of repeating itself. His description of America as a nation "so proverbially forward-looking, so universally deemed to be concerned only with the future, so faithful to the idea of progress," yet caught in an examination of its present and past, felt uncomfortably familiar.

I couldn't help but wonder: Had we truly progressed as a nation, or were we trapped in an endless cycle of repeating the same mistakes? When Beloff spoke of "traditional beliefs" failing to offset facts, of historic ideals receiving only "lip service," I saw the same struggles playing out in our current discourse on race, equality, and justice. His reflections on slavery—a blight on America's history that persisted despite the Founding Fathers' lofty ideals—mirrored the ongoing fight against systemic racism and inequality today.

The questions Beloff raised in 1948 about whether America's political habits and institutions had become obstacles to its ideals now felt more relevant than ever. The frightening present he spoke of seemed to be staring us in the face, daring us to confront the uncomfortable truth that progress is not guaranteed. His words weren't just a historical critique; they were a challenge to the present, a call to examine whether we are merely paying lip service to the ideals we hold dear or truly committed to making them a reality.

It was then that I understood: Beloff's article wasn't just a reflection on the past—it was a mirror held up to our present, urging us to reconcile the gap between our ideals and our realities. That gap, which Beloff identified so astutely, remains a chasm for many today. The promise of liberty and justice for all still feels distant for those marginalized by the very systems designed to protect and empower them. This realization hit me with a force I wasn't prepared for.

I finished the article and sat down, shaken. What did I just read? How could he be so spot on with so many of his observations? From the tense rhetoric and discourse that erupted when Colin Kaepernick kneeled on the football field to Derek Chauvin kneeling on the neck of George Floyd—two profoundly different acts of kneeling that altered the course of history in such starkly different ways—I found myself at an inflection point.

What began as mere curiosity had led to an epiphany. How did I get here? How did this Black kid from the South Side of Chicago manage to close the gap between his ideals early in life to create realities later in life, one step of faith at a time? How does one process and question their identity, their place in society, in the corporate world, and eventually in the political arena? How does one witness two men—Kaepernick and Chauvin—"take a knee" in two vastly different environments and circumstances, and arrive at this moment . . . by taking a knee myself, kneeling before my God, and choosing faith over fear?

The image of Kaepernick, kneeling silently during the national anthem to protest racial injustice, stands in stark contrast to Chauvin's violent act of kneeling on George Floyd's neck, an act that led to Floyd's death and ignited a global movement for justice. Both acts, though seemingly unrelated, are inextricably linked in their impact on society. One was a plea for recognition of the harsh realities that so many people of color face every day; the other, a brutal manifestation of those very realities.

As I grappled with the implications of Beloff's words and the events that had unfolded in my own lifetime, I couldn't help but see the parallels between the ideals that America has always claimed to stand for and the stark, painful realities that so many of us experience. These realities are not just historical footnotes; they are ongoing struggles that demand our attention and action.

But how do we bridge this gap? How do we turn ideals into

realities, not just in political rhetoric but in the lived experiences of every human being? This question took root in my mind, growing more persistent with each passing day.

I began to think about the many communities I had encountered throughout my life—communities that had been promised so much by politicians, yet had received so little. Communities where the American Dream felt like an illusion, a distant hope that was always just out of reach. These were the communities that had shaped me, that had taught me resilience and faith, even in the face of overwhelming odds.

Growing up, I had seen firsthand the disparities between the ideals we are taught to believe in and the realities we live in. My community was rich in culture, in history, in strength—but it was also a community that had been systematically marginalized, its needs ignored by those in power. The schools were underfunded, the streets were often unsafe, and opportunities were scarce. Yet, despite these challenges, there was a profound sense of hope, a belief that things could get better if we just kept pushing, kept fighting for what was right.

This belief in the possibility of change, in the power of faith, was instilled in me from a young age. It was what carried me through the toughest moments of my life, what kept me grounded when everything else seemed to be falling apart. It was this faith that led me to work on Joe Biden's presidential campaign, to fight for a vision of America that was more inclusive, more just, more aligned with the ideals we hold dear.

Even as I worked tirelessly on the campaign, I couldn't shake the feeling that, despite our best efforts, some people felt we were still falling short of the mark. The ideals were there, prominently displayed in every speech, every policy proposal, but the realities—those stubborn, unyielding realities—remained unchanged for too many.

As I reflected on these experiences, on the gap between ideals and realities, I realized that the key to bridging this gap lies not in grand gestures or sweeping reforms, but in the small, everyday actions we take. It lies in the choices we make, the conversations we have, the way we treat one another. It lies in the willingness to listen, to learn, to grow. And most important, it lies in the strength of our faith.

Faith is not just a belief in something greater; it is a call to action. It is the force that compels us to keep going, even when the odds are stacked against us. It is the courage to stand up for what is right, to speak out against injustice, to fight for those who cannot fight for themselves. It is the determination to turn our ideals into realities, no matter how difficult the path may be.

This is what I would run on, I thought. Not on empty promises or lofty ideals, but on the commitment to making those ideals a reality for everyone, regardless of their background, their circumstances, or their struggles. But as I reflected deeper, I began to realize something even more profound: It wasn't just about what I would be running for—it was about what I had been running from. I wasn't just running toward the vision of a better world; I had been running away from the unknown, from the uncertainty of what comes next when you step outside the comfortable boundaries of the roles you've always played. It hit me like a revelation: Sometimes the hardest thing isn't figuring out what you're called to do—it's letting go of what was so you can step into the promise of what could be. I had to face the truth that the clarity I was seeking wasn't just about what I wanted to create—it was about the fear of leaving behind what had already defined me for so long. This wasn't just a question of ambition or purpose—it was about confronting the fears that kept me tethered to what was safe, instead of stepping boldly into what I knew I was truly called to do.

I didn't know if I would ever actually run for office, but in that moment, it didn't matter. What mattered was the clarity that had come from asking the question, from seeking God's guidance, from reflecting on the lessons of the past and the challenges of the present. What mattered was the understanding that my purpose, my calling, was not just to dream of a better world but to work tirelessly to bring it into being.

That clarity also illuminated something I had been wrestling with for some time. The role I had played, first on the campaign and then as Chief Diversity and Inclusion Officer at the White House, had been both a profound honor and a tremendous responsibility. For nearly five years, I had been "on call," my life shaped by the needs and demands of the job—demands that didn't just fall on me but on my family as well. My wife, Brittany, and my twin daughters, Lela and Nia, had shared in the sacrifices, the late nights, the travel, and the phone calls and emails that never stopped. While I had poured my heart into the work, there were moments when I realized that the price of continuing down this path might be more than I was willing to pay.

It wasn't an easy decision. The weight of responsibility is heavy when you're in a role that feels as though it holds the power to change lives. The work we were doing mattered. It mattered deeply. I began to pay closer attention to the patterns in my life—the quiet whispers of God that had been tugging at my heart, reminding me that sometimes stepping into the unknown is the most faithful act we can take.

In those moments of reflection, I realized that the clarity I was seeking wasn't about running for office or staying in a prestigious role. It was about recognizing when it was time to move on, to trust the pull of a higher calling, and to make room for something new. The campaign and the White House had taught me invaluable lessons, but they had also consumed so much of me. It was time to step back, to create space for the next chapter, and to give more of myself to the things that truly mattered—my faith, my family, and my purpose beyond the title.

So, I made the decision. I let go of the role, trusting that the work I had done would carry on in the hands of others and that my path forward was guided by something greater than ambition or duty. I chose to move on, not because the work wasn't important, but because it was time to turn the page. The call to be present for my family, the desire to honor the patterns I had seen unfolding in my life, and the pull of God's voice all led me to this decision.

I didn't know exactly what the next chapter would hold, but I knew it was time. I knew that faith doesn't always show you the entire path—sometimes it simply asks you to take the next step.

As I sat in my home, the rain still tapping softly against the window, I felt a sense of peace wash over me. The doubts, the fears, the uncertainties—they were still there, but they no longer held the same power over me. I knew that whatever came next, I would face it with faith, with courage, and with the unwavering belief that we can turn our ideals into realities if we are willing to do the work.

I thought about the many people I had met along my journey— those who had inspired me, challenged me, and pushed me to be better. I thought about the communities that had raised me, the mentors who had guided me, the friends and family who had supported me. I realized that this was not just my journey; it was our journey. A journey that we are all on together, each of us contributing in our own way to the collective work of building a more just and equitable world. But as much as this journey has been about confronting the gaps between our ideals and our realities, it has also been about understanding the price we pay when we allow those gaps to persist—and the promises we unlock when we close them.

In every challenge we face, there is a price to be paid and a promise to be fulfilled. The price of division is the erosion of our shared humanity, but the promise of unity is the strength we find in coming together. The price of fear is the paralysis that keeps us from acting, but the promise of faith is the courage that propels us forward. The price of giving up is the surrender of our dreams, but the promise of moving on is the renewal of our hope. The price of clinging to potential alone is a life filled with unfulfilled promises, but the promise of following patterns is the steady progress that leads to real transformation. The price of choosing preference over purpose is the loss of deeper meaning, but the promise of purpose is a life aligned with a higher calling that moves us toward lasting impact.

As I reflect on these prices and promises, I can't help but think about how they resonate beyond my own journey. They speak to something universal—a quiet tension we all carry between the life we dream of and the one we live, between the ideals we hold and the realities we face. These moments of tension are not roadblocks; they are invitations to examine our lives, to question what truly matters, and to decide what we are willing to fight for.

This isn't about survival alone; it's about transformation. It's about finding the courage to face our fears, to confront the obstacles that stand in our way, and to embrace the promises that await on the other side of every challenge. The journey isn't easy, but it's worth it—because in every step forward, we uncover a deeper truth about who we are and who we're meant to become.

When I look back on the path that brought me here, I see the moments that shaped me—not just the triumphs, but the trials. I see how faith carried me through, how resilience was born from struggle, and how clarity emerged from the questions I was brave enough to ask. These lessons aren't just mine; they are reflections of a shared humanity, a collective story of hope, perseverance, and the relentless pursuit of something better.

I don't know where the road ahead will lead me, but I've learned this much: A person who kneels before God can stand before any-one. That, perhaps, is the most powerful promise of all—that no matter where you are or what you face, you can stand tall in the knowledge that you are never alone.

Fear often disguises itself as protection, convincing us to stay where we are, but the truth is, the life you've always imagined isn't beyond your reach—it's waiting for you to step toward it. What are the truths you've been running toward—or running from? The question isn't whether the bridge can be built; it's whether you're willing to take the first step across it.

It's not about being perfect. It's about being willing. Because sometimes all it takes is one person willing to believe, to hope, to step forward, and to trust that change is possible.

It only takes one.

Will you be the one?

Part II
Choices That Change Us

EVERY JOURNEY COMES WITH A COST. WHETHER IT'S THE pursuit of a dream, a fight for justice, or the decision to live with intention, there are always sacrifices to be made. The choices we make—what we hold on to, what we let go of, what we stand for—shape not only who we become as individuals, but who we become as a society. In my own life, I've faced moments where the price of moving forward felt overwhelming, and the temptation to settle for less was strong. I've also learned that for every price paid, there is a promise waiting on the other side—a promise of growth, clarity, and alignment with purpose.

The gap between our personal ideals and our realities, and the gap between the ideals we champion as a society and the reality we live, can feel insurmountable at times. But these gaps are where transformation happens. The choices we make in these moments determine whether we stay bound to patterns that no longer serve us or step forward into a greater version of ourselves. Do we cling to division, or do we pursue unity? Do we chase potential, or do we trust patterns? Do we choose preference, or do we surrender to purpose? These decisions define us. They define the world we create.

In the chapters that follow, we'll explore the costs of staying the same and the promises that come when we embrace change. Whether it's recognizing patterns over potential, making peace with letting go, or summoning the courage to take the step that changes everything—every choice shapes the future, both personally and collectively. Each section invites you to reflect on the choices that shape the course of our lives and the world around us.

The journey ahead is not just about facing challenges—it's about seeing the meaning behind them. It's about recognizing that the choices we make today are bridges to the future we hope for. My goal is simple: to provide you with the tools, insights, and principles you can apply in your own journey toward both personal and societal growth. I believe we each hold the power to close the gap between where we are and where we are meant to be, both in our personal lives and in the larger fabric of society. That power begins with the choices we make—the choice to pay the price, to trust the promise, and to move forward with faith.

As you read, I invite you to reflect on your own journey. What choices have shaped you? What decisions are still before you? What price are you willing to pay for the promise of something greater? My hope is that these pages will offer not just insight, but the encouragement to step into the life—and the world—you are called to build.

The journey won't always be easy. But the promise that awaits—for you, and for all of us—is worth every step.

CHAPTER 10

From Division to Unity

DIVISION DOESN'T START AS A WAR. IT STARTS AS A SPARK. A single offense, a passing remark, a misunderstanding left to smolder. At first, it's just smoke—barely noticeable, easy to dismiss. But left unchecked, that spark catches, spreads, and soon, what was once a small ember of disagreement becomes an unstoppable wildfire of separation, consuming relationships, communities, and even entire nations. History has shown us time and again: Division is the beginning of downfall. "United we stand, divided we fall" is more than just an old adage—it is a warning. A reminder that the greatest threats don't always come from the outside; often, they are the fires we fail to put out within.

Division and destruction are inseparable forces—one erodes, the other demolishes. The only difference is time. Division leads to distance, and distance creates distortion. Step far enough away from anything, and your vision blurs. A friend becomes a stranger. A teammate becomes an enemy. A neighbor becomes "them." The more distant we are from understanding one another, the more distorted our perceptions become. When we stop engaging with people who think differently, look differently, or live differently, we allow division to take root. The price of division? The breakdown of empathy, of understanding, and of growth.

In today's social and political climate, the cost of division is staggering. We see it in our communities, our workplaces, our homes. It fuels rhetoric that demonizes the "other side"—whether in political debates, racial conversations, or ideological differences in faith and culture. The more divided we become, the harder it is to listen, to learn, and to grow as individuals and as a collective society. Unity, however, offers a different promise—a promise that through understanding and collaboration, we can heal, evolve, and create a future that benefits us all.

I've seen this cycle play out not just in history or politics but in faith communities as well. One sermon that has stayed with me is from Pastor Steven Furtick, who spoke about the dangers of offense. He pointed out that people of faith often face attacks from the enemy, or as the church refers to it, "Satan." These attacks aren't always loud or obvious—they come subtly, in the form of offense, which quietly leads to division.

"The enemy's agenda is destruction, his strategy is division, and his tactic is offense," Furtick said. That struck me deeply because it captured a spiritual truth that plays out in every aspect of life—relationships, communities, and even nations. It starts small. Someone says or does something that offends us. We hold on to that offense, we nurture it, and over time, it grows. We stop communicating. We build walls instead of bridges, and before we know it, the divide is so wide that crossing it feels impossible.

This isn't just personal—it's systemic. Offense leads to division, and division, if left unchecked, leads to destruction. We've seen it in our politics, where division has become more than just a difference of opinion—it's become a driving force of separation and hostility.

The promise of unity is greater. It offers healing, progress, and strength. Community is critical to our well-being. Studies have shown that people who engage in healthy communities live longer, healthier lives. They experience lower levels of stress, depression, and isolation. Research conducted by Harvard's T. H. Chan School of Public Health found that strong social connections improve longevity, reduce the risk of premature death, and improve overall physical and mental health.

> *Community is critical to our well-being.*

The same principle applies on a broader scale. When people come together—whether in families, teams, workplaces, or nations—they create a collective strength that is far greater than the sum of its parts. Unity doesn't mean uniformity. It doesn't require that we all think the same or agree on every issue. Rather, it means that we come together with a shared purpose, even in the midst of our differences. There is a promise found in unity. We become stronger in numbers, louder in numbers, and more resilient in numbers. We are capable of traveling farther together than we ever could alone. Too often, people sabotage their own success by competing with those they were meant to collaborate with. Collaboration, in unity, is a powerful vehicle for driving progress forward.

In my years working with professional sports teams, I witnessed firsthand how division within a team could erode its culture and success faster than anything else. A locker room divided—whether through conflict between players or misalignment between leadership and staff—ultimately weakens the team's ability to perform.

You don't have to look far for proof of this. Even the most talented teams can crumble under division, while unity can turn great teams into dynasties. Take the 1990s Chicago Bulls—a team stacked with some of the best talent the game had ever seen. When

Dennis Rodman first joined the team, his individual brilliance on defense was undeniable, but his commitment to the system was shaky. It wasn't until he fully bought into the team's mission—trusting Phil Jackson's leadership and embracing his role alongside Michael Jordan and Scottie Pippen—that the Bulls became unstoppable, securing three straight championships from 1996 to 1998.

When a team operates in unity—trusting one another, communicating openly, and collaborating toward a common goal—the possibilities are limitless.

This same principle of unity was tested during a pivotal stretch of the 2024 presidential election cycle—a moment when division wasn't just present between opposing sides but ran deep within a collective that desperately needed cohesion. Leadership in that moment demanded an extraordinary choice, one that required stepping back for the sake of something larger than oneself.

In that moment, then-President Joe Biden made the courageous decision to step aside—not because he doubted his ability to lead, but because he understood that unity within the Democratic Party was more important than personal ambition. By endorsing then-Vice President Kamala Harris and clearing the way for her nomination, he offered a profoundly moving example of mission-first leadership—not because we didn't believe in him, but because he believed in us. Whether or not stepping aside sooner might have changed the outcome is a question we may never know—but what we do know is that his decision reflected the kind of leadership that values the mission above all else. It showed us that sometimes leading means trusting others to carry the torch forward.

That belief—the trust he placed in our ability to carry the mission forward—was a reminder that leadership isn't about holding on to power. It's about empowering others to rise, about stepping aside so the collective can thrive. It was a moment that demonstrated that unity requires not just courage, but faith in the people who make progress possible.

But what happens when division isn't just a leadership challenge—but a way of life? When it's not just a disagreement—but a design? This is where division becomes something deeper, something structural. It doesn't just strain relationships or weaken teams, it shapes entire realities. It influences who gets heard, who gets opportunities, and who gets left behind. It dictates who rises and who remains unseen.

Societal Unity

Division doesn't just exist within families or organizations—it's woven into the very fabric of society. The promise of unity isn't about erasing differences, it's about learning to live and thrive within them. The gap between American ideals—liberty, equality, justice for all—and our lived realities is wide. While progress has been made, ignoring the divides that still exist only pushes them deeper.

We tell ourselves a powerful story about America: that it is a land of opportunity, resilience, and self-made success. It's a good story, inspiring even. But it's not the whole story. For too long, we've treated success as if it exists in a vacuum, as though everyone starts the race from the same place and runs the same course. But America was built on a terrain that wasn't level. Some were given the clearest paths, paved with access and privilege. Others had to navigate rough terrain—boulders of discrimination, economic exclusion, and legal barriers—just to make it to the starting line.

Ignoring this doesn't promote fairness; it promotes ignorance. A national amnesia blinds us to the truth: Collective prosperity is impossible without acknowledging our uneven past.

Recognizing inequality isn't about assigning blame—it's about choosing to see the full picture. Too often, we assume that acknowledging disparities means accepting guilt. But in truth, it's about responsibility—and the possibility of something better.

Much of the opposition to DEI isn't about rejecting fairness—it's about fearing the unknown. When you've always had a head start, equality can feel like a disadvantage. I've had countless conversations with people who believed DEI was a threat to their sense of stability. What I learned is that their fear wasn't always about opposing fairness; it stemmed from the uncertainty of change. They worried that leveling the playing field meant they would lose what little advantage they had.

That fear, left unaddressed, leads to division. And division—whether in society or organizations—always comes at a price. That cost is progress lost, potential wasted, and a society that is weaker, not stronger.

But the promise of unity offers something greater than fear: It offers shared investment. Unity asks us to believe that what lifts one of us can lift all of us. It's not about lowering standards—it's about redefining excellence. True excellence isn't built by isolating talent; it's built by embracing the full spectrum of human potential.

When I hear people say that DEI initiatives are a threat to merit, I ask them: What kind of merit are we measuring? Because if merit exists in a vacuum, without accounting for the barriers some have faced and the privileges others have benefited from, then we're not measuring merit—we're measuring access.

Think of Serena Williams. No one questions her athletic dominance, but her achievements are made even more extraordinary when you consider the barriers she faced in a sport that wasn't built for her. Context doesn't diminish her greatness—it deepens it. The same is true for countless leaders, innovators, and change-makers whose paths were made steeper by systemic barriers. Acknowledging their journeys isn't making excuses—it's making sense of reality.

Historically, internal division has been the downfall of some of the greatest powers in the world. Rome didn't fall because it ran out of soldiers—it fell because it ran out of unity. The Soviet Union didn't collapse from outside pressure—it fractured from within. When nations allow internal divides to fester, innovation slows, economies weaken, and societal trust erodes.

America, in many ways, stands at that same crossroads today. While we argue over whether DEI helps or harms us, other nations are surging ahead in areas like AI, renewable energy, and technology. If we don't confront this internal division, we not only risk falling behind but staying behind—economically and in our ability to foster innovation and progress.

The truth is, division isn't just a political problem—it's an innovation problem, an economic problem, and a national security problem. Unity doesn't weaken a nation; it strengthens it by unlocking the potential of all its people.

As a nation, we must confront the reality that systems designed to protect certain interests can also become barriers to collective progress. James Clear, in *Atomic Habits*, puts it simply: "We don't rise to the level of our goals, we fall to the level of our systems." We can set all the aspirational goals about progress, but without systems that support them, they will remain just that—aspirations, not realities.

Unity doesn't happen by accident. It requires us to be intentional about breaking down the walls that division builds. What if we, as a society, chose to embrace faith over fear? What if we believed that our differences could be a source of strength, not a cause for division? What if we designed systems that created shared opportunities, rather than reinforced privilege?

DEI isn't about making anyone feel guilty or taking something away—it's about creating a stronger, more resilient future where everyone has a fair shot. We're at our best when we work together, combining perspectives, ideas,

> *Unity doesn't weaken a nation; it strengthens it.*

and experiences. Studies by McKinsey, Deloitte, and *Harvard Business Review* consistently show that diverse teams are more innovative, productive, and profitable. But beyond the data, this is about the America we claim to be.

Imagine an America where opportunity isn't determined by where you're born, what you look like, or how much your family earns. Imagine a future where we no longer see diversity as a "check-the-box" exercise but as a core ingredient for innovation and growth. That vision isn't just possible—it's necessary.

The Promise of Unity

The promise of unity isn't just about closing the gaps between us. It's about creating something larger—something that reflects the best of who we are and who we can become when we work together. It's a choice we must make, both individually and collectively. It requires us to confront the fear that divides us and choose to embrace the belief that we are stronger together than we are apart. This is not a simple task, nor is it comfortable. Unity demands that we listen to one another, that we engage in hard conversations, and that we acknowledge both the pain and the potential for healing. Division is the price we pay when we allow fear to drive our decisions. But unity offers us the chance to bridge the gap between our ideals and our realities, creating a society that values both individuality and collective strength.

This is true on every level—whether in your family, your workplace, your community, or your nation. Unity doesn't mean that we ignore our differences or pretend that our struggles don't exist. It means that we work through them together, recognizing that our collective strength comes from our ability to unite despite our differences. When we choose to bridge the gap, we create a nation where the best is always yet to come.

Bridging the Gap Between Division and Unity

How do we begin to foster unity in our own lives, in our communities, and in society at large? It starts with reflection and intentional action. Here are practical tools to help you assess and actively work toward unity, both personally and societally:

1. **Identify Areas of Division**
   - **Reflect:** Where has division taken root in your life? Are there conversations you've avoided, people you've written off, or situations where you've chosen comfort over clarity? Have you let offense or misunderstanding create distance between you and someone else? What bridges have you allowed to burn—and which ones are worth rebuilding?
   - **Action:** Write down one area where you've experienced division and commit to having a conversation or taking a step toward reconciliation.

2. **Embrace Empathy**
   - **Reflect:** Empathy is a key tool in fostering unity. Try to see the world through someone else's perspective,

especially those with whom you disagree or feel disconnected. What experiences might they have that
shape their views? How can you better understand
their pain, their fears, or their hopes?

- **Action:** This week, have a conversation with someone whose perspective challenges you. Instead of
preparing a response, sit in their story—listen to
their experiences, their struggles, their hopes. What
does it feel like to truly hear them?

3. **Seek Common Ground**
   - **Reflect:** Division often thrives because we focus on
   what separates us rather than what unites us. In your
   personal relationships, workplace, or community,
   actively seek out common ground. What shared
   values or goals can you build upon? What common
   hopes can you work toward, even if your paths to
   achieving them look different?
   - **Action:** Identify one common goal with someone
   who has a different perspective and commit to working toward it together.

4. **Acknowledge the Role of Fear**
   - **Reflect:** Fear is often at the root of division. Where
   has fear caused you to build walls instead of bridges?
   Have you ever avoided a conversation because you
   were afraid of being uncomfortable? Whether it's
   fear of change, fear of loss, or fear of being misunderstood, we must acknowledge the role that fear
   plays in our lives and in society. How has fear led
   you to retreat instead of reach out?

- **Action:** Write down one fear that has kept you from engaging with someone different from you. Now ask yourself: What's the worst that could happen if you faced it? What's the best that could happen if you overcame it?

5. **Commit to Being a Bridge-Builder**
   - **Reflect:** Think about the last time you witnessed division—in your workplace, your family, your community? Did you step in to mend it, or did you let it grow? What would it look like if, instead of walking away, you built a bridge?
   - **Action:** Find one person this week who needs a bridge—not just between ideas, but between people. Be intentional in creating a space where understanding can grow. It might be a conversation, an introduction, or a small act of reconciliation. Whatever it is—be the reason a connection happens.

As you consider what unity means in your own life, take a moment to pause and reflect. Where has division crept into your relationships, your community, or your perspective? How has it taken root, and what would it take to begin healing those fractures? Maybe it starts with a single conversation, or perhaps it requires stepping back to see the bigger picture. Think about the actions you can take—small or large—that might bridge the gap where division once stood. What shifts would occur if you chose empathy over judgment, understanding over assumptions, and connection over separation? Imagine what could change if you became intentional about fostering unity in your daily interactions.

This reflection doesn't have to be done alone. Consider exploring these questions in dialogue with others—at work, in your community, or among close friends. Unity doesn't just happen—it's built, moment by moment, conversation by conversation, bridge by bridge. When we share our experiences, our struggles, and our hopes, we amplify the impact. Together, we begin to build what division tried to destroy.

The Price and the Promise

The price of division is steep—it isolates us, weakens us, and keeps us from realizing our full potential. Whether in personal relationships or in the larger fabric of society, division prevents us from working toward the common good. It keeps us stuck in cycles of fear, misunderstanding, and disconnection.

But the promise of unity is greater. Unity isn't just a feel-good ideal, it's a choice to build something greater than ourselves. It invites us to move beyond our differences and find strength in our shared humanity. Unity is not about erasing our uniqueness—it's about celebrating it in the context of a greater purpose.

I encourage you to take the principles of unity to heart. Where are you holding on to division? What fears are driving that division? And how can you begin to foster unity in your personal life, your community, and in society?

Unity requires faith—faith in one another, faith in the promise of something greater, and faith that, when we come together, we are capable of creating a future that honors both our individuality and our collective strength. When we choose unity, we choose to believe that the best is yet to come—for ourselves, for our communities, and for the world around us.

Yet, to make unity a reality, we must also recognize the patterns that either support or undermine our potential for growth. Just as division can hold us back, so too can our reliance on potential without grounding ourselves in the consistent patterns that drive true progress. As we move forward, we must not only seek unity but also acknowledge the power of the patterns we follow—both in our lives and in society.

CHAPTER 11

Patterns Over Potential

WE'VE ALL BEEN THERE—CAPTIVATED BY SOMEONE OR SOME-
thing based on what it could become. A relationship. A career opportunity. A business venture. The potential was intoxicating. We
saw the vision, the promise, that what-if, and we ignored the patterns. That's how we get stuck. Not because we lack vision, but
because we trust potential more than patterns. Potential is a word
that speaks to what could be. It's full of promise, possibility, and
hope. It's the reason we take risks in relationships, careers, and
even our personal growth. Potential fuels our belief in what might
happen, in the untapped greatness that lies just beneath the surface. But as powerful as potential is, it's often not enough to bring
those ideals into reality. Why? Because potential alone isn't what
shapes our lives—it's patterns.

Patterns—the consistent behaviors, actions, and results that unfold over time—are what ultimately determine whether potential
will be fulfilled. While potential offers hope, patterns provide evidence. It's not that potential doesn't matter, but when we look at
the gap between our ideals and our realities, we have to confront a
critical truth: It's not potential that brings dreams to fruition; it's
patterns that tell us the truth about what will come to pass.

This concept plays out across all areas of life—whether it's in your career, your personal relationships, your faith journey, or your leadership roles. And when we allow potential to blind us to the patterns, the cost can be high.

Think about it: How many times have you been drawn to someone or something based on what it could become? Maybe it was a relationship, a new hire, or a business opportunity. You saw the potential and allowed it to fuel your hope. How often did you stop to consider the patterns? The patterns of behavior, the consistent outcomes, the ways in which this person or opportunity had repeatedly shown you who or what they really were?

I've experienced this firsthand at multiple points in my career. When I was at NFL headquarters, I often found myself faced with two things: the potential of what could happen if certain decisions were made, and the patterns of what had historically unfolded. One of the biggest lessons I learned was that potential, while exciting, is often unreliable without the grounding evidence of patterns. Patterns will teach you more about people, organizations, and even yourself than potential ever will.

This realization became even more important during my time at the White House. I worked with some of the brightest minds, and every day was full of the potential for major impact. However potential can be intoxicating—it makes you believe that if you just push a little harder, stay a little longer, something will finally shift. What I came to understand—particularly when wrestling with the decision to move on—was that the patterns were speaking louder than the possibilities. The habits of leadership. The way decisions were made. The repeated tensions that never fully resolved. Potential said, "Maybe if you just hold on a little longer . . ." but patterns said, "This is what it will always be."

It's easy to be captivated by potential because it gives us hope. But when you stop to look at the patterns, you gain clarity.

Patterns—whether in your career, relationships, or faith journey—show you where you're really headed.

This isn't just true for individuals—it's true for nations. America was founded on a set of powerful ideals: liberty, justice, equality for all. These ideals represent the potential of what the nation could become, but potential alone doesn't bridge the gap between what is and what could be. It's the patterns in society—policies, behaviors, historical cycles—that show us the reality.

America has always told itself a powerful story—about liberty, justice, and opportunity. But history tells a different story: that potential alone doesn't change realities. Patterns do. The pattern of exclusion. The pattern of inequity. The pattern of policies that reinforce privilege rather than dismantle it. If we keep clinging to what America *could* be without addressing what it *is*, we'll never close the gap between our ideals and realities.

History is full of moments when people ignored the signs, convinced that their vision of what could be was stronger than the reality of what was unfolding before them. One of the most well-known examples of this? The *Titanic*.

The *Titanic* didn't sink just because it hit an iceberg—it sank because multiple warnings were dismissed before the moment of impact. Engineers, captains, and decision-makers saw cracks in the system but believed the ship was "unsinkable." Their confidence in the ship's potential blinded them to the reality of the pattern: ignored safety measures, overlooked weaknesses, and the refusal to adapt when warning signals appeared.

How often do we do the same in our own lives? How many relationships, businesses, or even societal structures sink—not in an instant, but slowly—because the warning signs were ignored until disaster became inevitable? It's a pattern as old as time. Whether in personal choices, leadership, or the broader direction of a nation, the cost of ignoring patterns is collapse. The *Titanic* didn't just hit an iceberg—it was already sinking long before impact, and so it is with the patterns that shape our lives.

As citizens, as leaders, and as a society, we must pay attention to the patterns that shape our communities and our country. Patterns of exclusion, division, and inequality are evident when we look at the struggles of marginalized communities, historical injustices, and the cycles of social unrest. We cannot rely on potential alone to carry us forward. It's only by addressing these patterns—confronting them, changing them—that we can hope to close the gap between our nation's ideals and its realities.

I've often thought about how many of us make promises based on hope, yet when it's time to follow through, we perform according to fear. That tension between potential and patterns is something I've witnessed time and again. We make commitments—about relationships, about jobs, about our nation—with the best of intentions, fueled by the hope of what could be. Yet when faced with the reality of action, fear often nudges us back into familiar patterns.

In relationships, this is especially common. You see the potential in someone you love, and you hold on to that hope, believing that things will get better, that they'll change, that the best is yet to come. How many times do the patterns show you otherwise? It's in those moments that you have to ask yourself: Am I following potential or trusting the patterns?

As a leader or CEO, this shows up in the way you hire people based on their potential, but you overlook the patterns of behavior that don't align with the company's values. Or perhaps it's the potential you see in a business venture that blinds you to the fact that the patterns of the market are telling you something different.

Even in faith leadership, pastors and church leaders face this tension. They may see the potential in their congregation or their ministry staff, believing that with the right support, that potential will be fulfilled. But what happens when the patterns show inconsistency? A pastor can get caught up in what the church could become while ignoring the patterns of stagnation that are actually holding it back.

The cost is often steep when we ignore patterns and continue to chase potential. When you invest in potential without paying attention to the patterns, you end up in a cycle of frustration, unmet expectations, and disappointment. In relationships, this looks like continually excusing behavior because you believe in what someone could become. In leadership, this looks like constantly giving chances to team members who never quite deliver but whose potential keeps you holding on.

The price of following potential blindly is that you may miss the reality that the patterns are trying to reveal. The danger is that we do this in all areas of life: careers, relationships, churches, businesses.

In my own life, I faced this multiple times. When I was with the Chicago Bears and later the NFL, I was driven by the potential of the impact I could make. But over time, the patterns began to reveal something else. There were limitations to what could be achieved, and staying would have meant sacrificing my growth for the sake of potential. The same was true when I was at the White House. The potential for impact was immense, but the patterns in the organization made me realize that my season there had come to an end. Moving on wasn't giving up—it was recognizing the patterns telling me it was time for the next chapter.

But here's the other side: When you start paying attention to patterns, you begin to make decisions based on reality, not fantasy. The promise of following patterns is clarity, growth, and sustainable success. Whether it's in a relationship, your faith journey, or your career, following patterns allows you to trust the direction you're heading.

In business, recognizing patterns helps you hire the right people, not based on potential but on proven behavior. In leadership,

> *When you start paying attention to patterns, you begin to make decisions based on reality, not fantasy.*

following patterns helps you discern when someone is truly growing or when it's time to make a change. In relationships, patterns help you build trust because actions, over time, speak louder than words.

Even in my faith journey, I've learned to recognize God's patterns in my life. When I've trusted those patterns—when I've followed where He's consistently led me—my faith has grown, and I've seen His promises fulfilled. When you make room for God, God will create rooms for you—new spaces and opportunities you never imagined. Recognizing His patterns in my life has always led me to deeper levels of trust, and it's helped me walk in the promise of His purpose.

Practical Steps:
How to Discern Potential from Patterns

How do you begin to trust patterns more than potential? How do you discern whether you're holding on to a vision that's no longer realistic, or whether the patterns are telling you it's time to move on? Here are some practical steps to help you.

1. **Track the Consistency of Behavior**

   Patterns reveal themselves over time. Take a step back and observe: What are the consistent behaviors you're seeing, whether in a person, an organization, or yourself? Ask yourself: *What has history shown me?*

2. Evaluate the Red Flags

We all see red flags early, but we often ignore them because we're fixated on potential. Take an honest look at the red flags you've noticed. Ask yourself: *What patterns are these red flags revealing?* Remember that red flags are often signals of deeper patterns—take time to evaluate what they might be pointing to.

3. Ask for Outside Perspective

Sometimes we're too close to the situation to see clearly. Seek out wise counsel—mentors, friends, or trusted advisors—who can help you see the patterns that you might be missing.

4. Balance Hope with Reality

Hope is powerful, but it must be balanced with evidence. Ask yourself: *Is there actual growth and change happening, or am I clinging to a vision of what could be?* Let your hope inspire you, but make sure it's grounded in what you've seen.

5. Consider Your Own Patterns

Often, we get stuck because of our own repeated behaviors. Reflect on your life and decisions. What are your patterns in responding to challenges? Are you repeating the same mistakes, expecting a different outcome? Patterns in your own behavior may be preventing you from seeing the truth and making necessary changes.

6. Recognize the Role of Faith

Faith plays a significant role in recognizing and trusting patterns. In your spiritual journey, observe where

God has led you before. Are there patterns of growth, provision, or guidance that you can trust to continue? Faith isn't about blindly following potential—it's about trusting that the patterns God has established in your life will guide you toward His purpose. Be patient as these patterns unfold.

Reflect: After going through these steps, what patterns have emerged, and how does this new understanding inform your next decision? Reflect on how this clarity will guide your future steps.

In the end, the real question is this: Are you willing to trust the patterns that life, God, and your experiences have revealed? It's easy to get caught up in potential because it offers so much hope. But when you let go of the blind pursuit of potential and start following the patterns—whether in relationships, careers, or faith—you begin to see the truth more clearly. The price of chasing potential without recognizing patterns is frustration and disappointment. However the promise of following patterns is growth, clarity, and alignment with your true purpose. Patterns are the signposts that show you where to go.

This is also true when we think about the broader societal patterns around us. Just like in our personal lives, America as a society has great potential, but what we often fail to address are the patterns of inequality, division, and exclusion that hold us back from fully realizing the ideals that are at the heart of this nation.

If we are to bridge the gap between American ideals and American realities, we must look to the patterns of history, governance, and social behavior. The ideals of freedom, equality, and justice will remain distant dreams unless we confront the patterns that perpetuate division, inequality, and injustice. Whether it's in how we engage with racial equity, the economy, or even in how we vote, the evidence of patterns must be acknowledged if we are to create real change. We cannot continue to chase the potential of what this country could be while ignoring the patterns that have held us back for so long. The promise of closing the gap between American ideals and realities rests in recognizing and transforming the patterns that dictate how we live and treat one another as a society. When we follow patterns that uplift, include, and create growth for everyone, we move closer to realizing the potential of a truly just and equitable society.

We've explored how the tension between potential and patterns shapes our world, but this principle is just as vital when applied to our personal lives. I've spent countless moments reflecting on this in my own journey—asking myself hard questions about whether I was clinging to potential or being honest about the patterns unfolding around me. What I've learned is that clarity often comes through intentional evaluation.

Clarity often comes through intentional evaluation.

Over time, I developed a framework for reflection—an exercise that helped me gain the clarity I needed to discern between hope and reality, between potential and patterns. Now, I want to offer you a tool to do the same. Whether you're evaluating a job, a relationship, a leadership role, or a personal pursuit, this exercise will help you take an honest look at whether you are grounded in proven patterns or caught up in wishful potential. This tool is simple but powerful: It asks you to step back, reflect, and recognize whether you're moving forward on solid ground or chasing something that hasn't yet materialized.

Tool: Am I Following Potential or Patterns?

INSTRUCTIONS

Think of a situation you're evaluating—this could be your career path, a relationship, a personal project, or even your faith journey. For each question below, choose either "Potential" or "Pattern" based on what feels most true for you right now.

- At the end, count how many times you selected "Potential" vs. "Pattern."
- While both potential and patterns play a role in decision-making, this tool will help you assess whether you're relying too heavily on hopes without evidence or grounding your actions in consistent patterns.

Potential vs. Patterns Evaluation

Question	Potential	Pattern
1. Do you find yourself focused on hopes for the future rather than recognizing the patterns of what is actually happening?	☐ Yes	☐ No
2. Do you find yourself justifying lack of progress by clinging to what "could be"?	☐ Yes	☐ No
3. Are there recurring issues you've ignored because of the potential for change?	☐ Yes	☐ No
4. Do you make decisions based on a future that hasn't yet materialized?	☐ Yes	☐ No
5. Are you seeing evidence of consistent behaviors or patterns that guide your decision-making?	☐ No	☐ Yes

COUNT YOUR RESPONSES

- Number of "Potential" selections:
- Number of "Pattern" selections:

INTERPRETATION OF YOUR RESULTS

If you have more "Potential" selections

You're likely holding on to future hopes rather than the reality of established patterns. This might mean you're focusing too much on what could be and not enough on what is. While potential can be inspiring, it's important to assess the consistent behaviors and outcomes to guide your decisions. Reflect on whether fear or comfort is preventing you from acknowledging the patterns, and consider grounding yourself in what's proven to be true.

If you have more "Pattern" selections

You are already focused on the reality of the situation and using patterns as your guide. This suggests you're aligned with making faith-based decisions grounded in truth. However, don't forget that a healthy balance between potential and patterns is necessary for growth—be sure to leave room for hope and vision as you move forward.

SCORING INTERPRETATION

0–2 "Potential" selections

You trust patterns and have a strong sense of discernment. This provides stability, but be mindful that too much caution can sometimes limit growth. Is there room to dream bigger? Reflect on whether you are leaving space for faith, vision, and possibility.

3–4 "Potential" selections

You're in the middle of the spectrum—balancing past lessons with future hope. However, take a moment to ask: Are there areas where you are holding on to potential that has no real evidence? Or, are there places where you're afraid to step into the unknown? This is a moment for deeper discernment.

5 "Potential" selections

You may be holding on to potential without recognizing the patterns in front of you. Ask yourself: What consistent evidence have I seen? What am I afraid to admit? It may be time to release old hopes and embrace the reality that God is showing you.

NEXT STEPS

Your results aren't meant to discourage you—they are meant to guide you. Whether you found yourself clinging to potential or fully trusting patterns, the next step is to act with clarity.

- **If "Potential" outweighs "Pattern," ask yourself:**
  - » What patterns have I been ignoring, and how can I begin focusing on reality rather than what might be?
  - » Write down one action step you can take to shift your focus toward patterns that will help guide your decision-making.

- **If "Pattern" outweighs "Potential," reflect on:**
  - » How this reality is informing your next steps, and whether there's room for more vision in your decisions.
  - » Write down one action step based on this pattern to move forward with confidence and clarity.

- **Deeper Reflection:** If you find yourself clinging to potential, ask yourself, "What fears are driving me to hold on to hopes rather than face the patterns?" Spend some time reflecting on the obstacles that may be preventing you from embracing the truth of your situation.

Faith in the Patterns

Remember this: Faith isn't just about believing in the potential of what could be—it's about trusting the patterns God has already laid out before you. In those patterns, you'll find the clarity, strength, and direction you need to move forward.

The patterns of consistency, faithfulness, and growth—these are the signposts that show you the path God has prepared for you. When you stop chasing potential and start honoring the patterns, you allow yourself to step into the promise of something far greater than you could have imagined.

In your personal life, your career, your relationships, and your spiritual walk—trust the patterns. When you do, you'll find that the gap between your ideals and your realities begins to close, and the path toward fulfilling your true potential becomes clearer. The price of chasing potential is that you may never see the reality of your ideals come to life. But the promise of following patterns is that they will guide you to the place where faith, purpose, and reality align. The patterns will always show you the way—if you're willing to see them and trust in the path they reveal.

Take the time to reflect on your life, your relationships, your career, and your faith. Look for the patterns. They will always point you toward truth, and when you follow them, you'll be stepping into the fullness of God's promise for your life.

As you prepare to step forward, remember that not all patterns are equal. Romans 12:2 (NIV) reminds us, "Do not conform to the pattern of this world, but be transformed by the renewing of your mind." This verse speaks to the patterns that often pull us away from truth—the patterns of fear, self-centeredness, and distractions that cloud our purpose. But when we turn to God, the patterns in our lives begin to reflect His plan and faithfulness. These divine patterns—marked by consistency, grace, and growth—become a blueprint for the journey ahead. Trusting those patterns isn't about conforming to the world; it's about aligning with the purpose God has laid before you.

God's patterns—His whispers in the quiet moments, His provision in seasons of doubt, His guidance in times of uncertainty— are always there, waiting for us to notice. When we stop chasing fleeting potential and start honoring the patterns, we allow ourselves to step into the promises He has prepared for us.

Trust the patterns:

> They will tell you where you're headed.
> They will tell you what's possible.
> They will tell you what must change.

The price of chasing potential is that you may never see the reality of your ideals come to life.

But the promise of following patterns?

> It's clarity.
> It's growth.
> It's stepping fully into God's purpose for you.

CHAPTER 12

Choosing Purpose Over Preference

WHICH IS MORE IMPORTANT: THE LIFE YOU IMAGINE FOR yourself or the life you were created to live? This question may seem simple, but for many, it's one that defines the path they walk every day. It's a question of preference versus purpose. It's not just personal—it's societal. Are we, as individuals and communities, chasing our preferences, or are we stepping into the purpose God has laid out for us?

Preferences are comforting. They make us feel safe, in control, and tethered to something familiar. But the longer we cling to our preferences, the further we may find ourselves from the purpose that was designed for us. Purpose, unlike preference, demands more from us—it requires surrender, trust, and faith.

I learned this lesson, not without difficulty, but with profound transformation. It's a lesson I want you to reflect on because the price of holding on to your preferences can be far greater than the discomfort of stepping into your purpose.

There was a time when my career in the NFL felt like the pinnacle of my professional aspirations. It was the manifestation of my personal preferences—what I wanted for my life. I climbed the ranks, worked in an organization I admired, and envisioned my future continuing within that world. I had a strong desire to be an NFL team president or perhaps even the commissioner one day. It made sense. It was familiar, but God had other plans.

The preference to stay in sports was strong—it felt like the right thing at the time, but the purpose that God had in mind was larger than what I could see. God's pull was undeniable, and after much prayer, reflection, and surrender, I made the decision to step into something I had never done before: politics.

There is a cost to clinging to your preferences, and I had to confront that. I had spent years climbing a "ladder" that felt comfortable, stable, and secure—until leadership expert John C. Maxwell's challenge stopped me in my tracks: "What good is climbing a ladder, year after year, only to reach the top and realize it's been leaning against the wrong building the entire time?" His words hit me like a ton of bricks.

This wasn't just a career decision. This was a life decision. The ladder I had been climbing was about preference—what felt good, what looked successful to the outside world. But purpose? That was something different altogether. Purpose required me to change the building my ladder leaned against, to stop confusing my preference with God's plan for me.

The tension between preference and purpose is real, and it's something we all experience. It's a struggle that transcends individual lives and extends to entire societies. Our preferences—whether in our personal lives, communities, or nations—can lead us down paths that feel productive but are ultimately misaligned with our true purpose.

Think about it: How often do we build entire systems—whether political, social, or economic—based on preference rather than principle? A modern example of this tension can be found in the growing debates around environmental sustainability. For decades, entire industries and economic systems have been built on the preference for convenience, profit, and short-term gain. The use of fossil fuels, single-use plastics, and unsustainable agricultural practices became entrenched because they offered immediate benefits to certain groups and industries. These preferences, while profitable and familiar, came at the cost of long-term environmental degradation and climate change.

Today, the global conversation has shifted toward purpose—rethinking how we treat the planet and moving toward sustainable practices that honor both the environment and future generations. This shift is not easy. It requires businesses and societies to let go of preferences rooted in convenience and economic comfort in favor of a larger, more meaningful purpose: the preservation of our planet. The resistance to change is often grounded in fear—fear of economic loss, fear of uncertainty, and fear of stepping into uncharted territory. The promise of embracing purpose over preference is clear. By shifting toward sustainable practices, we create a future that aligns with the principles of stewardship, responsibility, and justice for future generations. It's a reminder that true progress happens when we let go of what's easy in favor of what's right.

====

Oprah Winfrey once shared a story that profoundly changed the way I understand surrender. At a pivotal moment in her career, she deeply desired the role of Sofia in Steven Spielberg's *The Color Purple*. It was more than just a job—it was a personal and professional dream. Oprah believed this role was destined for her and poured her heart into her prayers and preparation. Despite her passion, uncertainty about the outcome weighed heavily on her. Doubt began to creep in, and she questioned whether her dream would ever come to fruition.

Seeking clarity and peace, Oprah decided to step away for a spiritual retreat. During that time, she found solace in singing the hymn "I Surrender All." In that moment, she realized she needed to let go of her desire to control the outcome and place her trust in God's plan. Reflecting on this experience, she has said that surrendering her deepest hopes allowed her to fully embrace the belief that what was meant for her would find its way to her.

Then the call came. Steven Spielberg had chosen her for the role. That moment of surrender not only led to her breakout performance in *The Color Purple*, but it also became a cornerstone of her spiritual philosophy: God's purpose for her life was far greater than anything she could have imagined. Her journey reminded me of the importance of surrender. True surrender isn't about giving up; it's about giving over—to God, to His purpose, and to His timing. When Oprah let go of her preferences, she stepped into a life far greater than the one she had planned, and the same is true for us.

Just as Oprah's story demonstrates the power of surrender, I've experienced firsthand how faith, trust, and genuine connection can open doors you could never predict. Let me take you back to one of those moments—courtside seats, a green room full of greatness, and a conversation that left an imprint on my soul.

One of the most memorable nights of my life started courtside at Madison Square Garden, watching the New York Knicks take on the Memphis Grizzlies alongside comedian JB Smoove, best known for his role in Larry David's hit show *Curb Your Enthusiasm*. JB and I had connected at an NFL event months earlier, and our genuine friendship led to nights like this—moments I couldn't have predicted but that felt perfectly aligned.

The game was electric, the kind of atmosphere only New York can deliver. But what made that night unforgettable had nothing to do with the final score. JB had invited me to join him afterward at legendary comedian Chris Rock's opening night for his Total Blackout tour at the Theater at MSG. After the show, Chris invited us to his green room—a space buzzing with energy and filled with some of the biggest names across entertainment and music. I had no idea that what awaited me inside would leave a lasting impact.

The energy in that green room was palpable. It was one of those spaces where greatness gathered, the kind you don't stumble into by accident but find yourself in when you're living in alignment with your purpose. Questlove, the legendary drummer of the Roots and Oscar-winning film director, was there, casually sharing stories. Rihanna, the globally celebrated pop icon and business mogul, held court effortlessly. Her presence commanded attention without a word needing to be said. Comedian and actor Aziz Ansari, then at the height of his fame with the Emmy-winning *Master of None*, was there, too, adding to the vibrant energy of the room. But it was my unexpected encounter with Trevor Noah, the South African comedian and then-host of *The Daily Show*, that left the deepest impression.

As we talked, Trevor shared the story of how Jon Stewart—the brilliant satirist and former host of *The Daily Show* at the time, who had redefined late-night political comedy—first reached out to him, slowly, over time, encouraging him to come to America and eventually step into the role of host of *The Daily Show*. Trevor admitted that he hadn't been actively pursuing this opportunity. There was no master plan. But when Jon saw something in him, it changed the trajectory of his life. "Sometimes," Trevor said, "you don't go looking for the moment—the moment finds you."

It wasn't just what Trevor said, but how much it reflected the very nature of faith. Faith isn't about mapping every step—it's about being ready when the moment finds you. That night reminded me that when you genuinely connect with people, with purpose, and with yourself, doors open in ways you could never script.

The courtside seats, the green room, and the conversation with Trevor Noah weren't about luck—they were about alignment. JB inviting me to the game, Chris Rock welcoming us backstage, and the serendipitous encounter with Trevor were reminders that faith and genuine connections can usher you into rooms where purpose reveals itself. But it's not just about being in the room—it's about being prepared for what happens when you get there.

What Trevor's story highlighted—and what my own journey confirmed—is that preparation meets purpose when we trust the process, release control, and remain open to what's meant for us. That night wasn't about chance. It was a living example of what happens when you surrender your preference and embrace the power of purpose. The relationships we cultivate, the faith we carry, and the willingness to act when called upon are what ultimately lead us to the places and opportunities we're meant to experience. In those moments, you find yourself exactly where you need to be, even when you don't expect it.

Purpose isn't about chasing opportunities—it's about being prepared for them. That night was a lesson in what happens when we let go of trying to control every outcome and instead trust that God will orchestrate the right encounters at the right time. The real challenge isn't in recognizing those moments—it's in surrendering long before they arrive.

God cannot establish what we have not surrendered. Whether it's our careers, relationships, or deeply held desires, surrender is the key that unlocks purpose.

> *Purpose isn't about chasing opportunities—it's about being prepared for them.*

The Power of Purpose

Purpose is not a destination; it's a journey. It's not something we arrive at; it's something we live into every day. When you align your life with God's purpose, you open the door to possibilities far greater than your preferences could ever offer. Purpose grounds us in something bigger than ourselves and shifts our focus from temporary preferences to lasting impact.

The promise of purpose is fulfillment. It's waking up every day knowing that you are exactly where you're supposed to be, doing exactly what you were meant to do. It's living a life where every step is ordered by God, where even the struggles have meaning, and where every sacrifice is part of the bigger picture.

When I walked away from the NFL and into the unknown world of political campaigns and the White House, I didn't have all the answers, but I had faith. Faith that purpose, not preference, was guiding me. And that faith, that trust in God's plan, led me to places I could never have dreamed of on my own.

Societies and nations, like individuals, also struggle with preference and purpose. If we're not careful, we can build entire communities, institutions, and systems based on preference—what's easy, comfortable, or traditional—rather than what's just, purposeful, and right.

America, like many countries, often finds itself grappling with this tension. We have ideals of liberty, equality, and justice, but the realities of inequality, division, and injustice remain. Why? Because too often we choose the comfort of familiar systems over the courage to pursue transformational change.

The challenge before us is this: Can we collectively surrender our preferences to align our society with its higher purpose? Can we, as a nation, let go of outdated preferences for power, control, and division and step into a purpose grounded in unity, justice, and equality?

The answer lies in the collective will to choose faith over fear, to trust that by letting go of what's comfortable, we can step into something far greater.

As a nation, we must ask ourselves: Is our ladder leaning against the wrong building? Are we climbing higher and higher, only to find that we've built systems that don't serve our people, our communities, or our world in the way they should? And if the answer is yes, are we willing to do the hard work of dismantling those ladders and building new ones, aligned with purpose, not preference?

Practical Steps: Choosing Purpose Over Preference

Here's how you can begin the journey of choosing purpose over preference—whether in your personal life or in the broader context of your community.

1. **Acknowledge Your Preferences:** Start by identifying the areas in your life where you're clinging to comfort or familiarity. What are you afraid of letting go?

2. **Surrender to God's Will:** Surrender doesn't happen overnight. It's an ongoing process. Through prayer, reflection, and seeking wisdom from others, begin to release control and trust God's purpose.

3. **Seek God's Purpose:** Ask God to show you what His purpose for your life is. This may come through prayer, scripture, or life experiences. Be open to receiving guidance in unexpected ways.

4. **Take Action in Faith:** Once you have clarity on your purpose, move toward it. It won't always be easy, but trust that God will guide each step.

5. **Check Your Ladder:** Reflect on whether you've been climbing the right ladder. Is it leaning against the right building? If not, don't be afraid to shift direction and pursue something that aligns with your purpose.

Moving from Reflection to Action

Stepping from preference to purpose requires courage, self-awareness, and faith. But the shift doesn't start with action—it starts with clarity. Before you take action, take a moment to pause. Where in your life has comfort held you back? Where have you chosen familiarity over faith? Reflection isn't about regret—it's about clarity.

This is your invitation to step into that space. Take a moment to consider the areas of your life where preferences may be guiding your choices. What might shift if you surrendered those preferences and leaned into God's purpose for you? Here are some prompts to help you reflect and move forward with intention:

• What are you holding on to?
  Name the places where comfort, control, or fear of change might be keeping you from stepping forward. It could be a job, a relationship, or a dream you've been afraid to pursue. Write them down—not as burdens, but as the starting point for transformation.

- When have you felt most aligned with your purpose?

    Reflect on the times when you've felt deeply connected to your higher purpose. What were you doing? Who was with you? What values were you living out? These moments are more than memories; they are clues that guide you toward your calling.

- Is your ladder leaning against the right building?

    Imagine spending years climbing a ladder—only to realize it's leaning against the wrong building. You've worked hard, sacrificed, and pushed forward, but are you climbing toward purpose or just a place of comfort? Think about your job, the organization you've built, the board you serve on, the relationships you invest in, the causes you champion, the family responsibilities you carry, or the dreams you've put on hold: Are these pursuits aligned with your true purpose, or have they become destinations of familiarity? The real question isn't just about where you're climbing but why. Are you pursuing a vision that's truly yours or one shaped by external expectations? If something inside you says your ladder is resting against the wrong building: Pause. Reflect. Realign. It's never too late to shift toward the purpose that brings true meaning and fulfillment.

- What action can you take today?

    Purpose isn't found all at once—it's discovered in the steps we take. What's one small but meaningful action you can take today to align your life more closely with God's purpose? Taking one action step that will help you move from preference to purpose is all it takes to start living the life you were destined for.

Tool: Purpose vs. Preference Self-Assessment

Are you walking in purpose—or just walking in circles? We all face moments where we question whether we're pursuing the life we were made for or settling into what feels safe. This self-assessment is more than just a set of questions—it's an opportunity to pause and reflect on whether your choices are guided by a deeper purpose or tethered to familiar preferences. It's a mirror. A checkpoint. A chance to see if your decisions are moving you forward or keeping you stuck.

Be honest. Your future depends on it.

INSTRUCTIONS

For each statement below, rate yourself on a scale from 1 to 5. Be honest about where you stand today. After answering all five statements, add up your total score and use it to reference the results section below to see where you currently stand.

1. How often do you make decisions based on what feels safe or familiar rather than what challenges you to grow?
   1 - Almost Always
   2 - Often
   3 - Sometimes
   4 - Rarely
   5 - Not at All

2. When faced with a difficult decision, do you lean more toward staying in your comfort zone or taking a step toward something uncertain but meaningful?

    1 - Comfort Zone
    2 - Mostly Comfort Zone
    3 - Somewhat Balanced
    4 - Mostly Toward Meaning
    5 - Toward Meaning

3. Do your daily habits reflect a commitment to long-term purpose or short-term comfort?
    1 - Short-Term Comfort
    2 - Mostly Comfort
    3 - Balanced Between Both
    4 - Mostly Purpose
    5 - Long-Term Purpose

4. Are there areas in your life—career, relationships, faith—where you feel stuck because of fear or resistance to change?
    1 - Definitely
    2 - Often
    3 - Sometimes
    4 - Rarely
    5 - Not at All

5. How aligned do you feel with your sense of purpose on a daily basis?
    1 - Not at All
    2 - Rarely
    3 - Sometimes
    4 - Often
    5 - Completely Aligned

TOTAL: _____

SCORING

5–12 Points (Fear-Based/Preference-Driven)

You're holding on more than you're letting go. Fear of change might be keeping you stuck. Identify one step—just one—that will move you closer to purpose this week. Name it. Commit to it. Your future depends on small, intentional steps of faith.

13–18 Points (Mixed Alignment)

You're making progress but something is still tethering you to familiarity. What's one thing you're afraid to release? Is it control? Comfort? Approval? Write it down—and challenge yourself to loosen your grip. Growth begins when we stop clinging to what no longer serves us.

19–25 Points (Purpose-Driven)

You are walking in purpose. You've chosen alignment over avoidance, faith over fear. Keep refining, keep growing, and keep surrendering what doesn't serve you. Now, who can you help? The next step in your journey isn't just about you—it's about using your purpose to guide others toward theirs.

As you assess where you may still be holding on to preferences, it's important to remember that stepping into purpose isn't always a clear or immediate path. Sometimes it requires walking into the unknown with faith.

What would it look like if you surrendered your preference for God's purpose? What doors could open, what transformation could happen, if you stopped trying to control the outcome and let God take the lead?

I've lived this truth. I've seen firsthand what happens when you let go of your preferences and step into the purpose God has for you. The path ahead isn't always clear, and sometimes it feels like you're walking into the unknown. But in that unknown, there is a promise—God's promise—that His purpose will lead you to places you never imagined.

===

Just as this principle of purpose applies to our personal lives, it also holds true at the societal level. Communities, cities, and nations often choose the familiar paths, the comfortable systems, rather than pursuing bold and transformative change.

When we cling to societal preferences—whether in politics, economics, or social structures—we limit our collective potential. We remain stuck in outdated systems that serve some but exclude many.

What if, as a society, we chose purpose over preference? What if we committed to building systems that reflect the values we claim to hold—liberty, equality, justice for all? It's easy to cling to the familiar, to the systems and structures that have always been in place. These preferences often reflect a fear of the unknown, a reluctance to step into something new.

The promise of purpose at the societal level is progress, unity, and the fulfillment of our highest ideals. However that promise will never be realized if we continue to cling to the preferences that divide us, that prioritize comfort over justice, and that maintain the status quo rather than challenging it.

===

Purpose is a journey that requires faith, trust, and surrender. It's not always easy to let go of the familiar, but when you do, you open yourself up to the fullness of what God has for you. You step into the life you were always meant to live.

The choice between preference and purpose is one we all must make, both individually and as a society. And the truth is, whatever you are not changing, you are choosing. If you continue to cling to your preferences, you are choosing to limit your potential, to live a life that may look successful on the outside but feels empty on the inside. But if you choose purpose, you are choosing a life of alignment, fulfillment, and transformation.

So, the question is simple: Will you continue to climb the ladder of your preferences, or will you shift your focus and climb toward the purpose God has for you?

God never calls you to less—only to more. But you cannot receive the more He has for you while clinging to what no longer serves you. The question is not if He has a plan—the question is will you trust it?

> *God never calls you to less— only to more.*

CHAPTER 13

The Price of Holding On and the Promise of Letting Go

LIFE IS FULL OF CROSSROADS—MOMENTS WHEN WE ARE faced with the choice to hold on or let go. The decisions we make in those moments shape the course of our lives in ways we often don't fully grasp until much later. In many cases, what we perceive as "giving up" might actually be the necessary step toward growth. And at other times, what we label as perseverance might be a disguise for fear—fear of the unknown, of failure, or of change.

The journey of knowing when to give up and when to move on is one of the hardest, most personal, and most deeply transformative experiences we face. That was certainly the case for me when I left the White House and entered the unknown. For months, I wrestled with the idea of leaving, unsure if it was the right time or if I had more to contribute. There was a part of me that was tempted to stay out of a sense of loyalty, out of a desire to fulfill what I believed was my purpose there. But there were signs—repeated signals from conversations, sermons, and moments of reflection— that pointed me in another direction. One of the most profound confirmations I received came through a sermon by Pastor Steven

Furtick, in which he talked about holding on to "the old thing" in our lives for too long.

He said something that hit me like a revelation: If you hold on to the *old thing* too long—how "it" was, what you wanted, how it was supposed to go in your mind—you might miss today's miracle trying to hold on to yesterday's blessing. That truth pierced through all the confusion I had been feeling. It's easy to hold on to something familiar, but if we hold on too long, we run the risk of missing what's next. Moving on is not the same as giving up; sometimes it's the only way to grow into what's waiting for us.

> *You cannot change what you will not confront.*

Acknowledging the moment is crucial. When faced with a significant decision, the first step is to confront it head-on. You cannot change what you will not confront. Growth demands honesty, and you will never grow if you refuse to face the reality of where you are. Yet many of us avoid this moment of truth, brushing past feelings of discontent, fear, or unease because facing them requires a level of vulnerability we aren't comfortable with. But here's the truth: Transformation begins the moment you stop avoiding the tension, lean into it, and embrace where you are as the starting point for where you're meant to go.

Think of it like a navigation system—when you're using a GPS, the first thing it requests is your starting location. You can't get to where you want to go until you've established where you are. The same is true with acknowledgment. It's like setting the "starting address" in your life's journey. Without understanding and accepting your present reality, you'll never be able to get clear directions on how to reach your destination. Avoidance doesn't protect you—it misguides you. You might have a vision of where you want to be, but until you confront where you are right now, your steps forward will be directionless, like trying to get somewhere without any guidance.

Acknowledging the situation isn't the end—it's only the beginning. The problem is that many people acknowledge a challenge and then stop there, thinking that awareness alone is enough. They get stuck in a cycle of reflection but never take action and that's where the real danger lies. As I often say to leaders, acknowledgment is a starting point, not a stopping point.

The moment you acknowledge that something needs to change, whether it's a relationship, a job, or even a mindset, is the moment you open yourself to new possibilities. But this is where most people falter. They get stuck in the awareness of the problem and are overwhelmed by the enormity of what comes next. That's where fear creeps in—the fear of giving up, the fear of losing something familiar, the fear of moving into uncharted territory.

The same is true for closing the gap between personal ideals and realities. You can't make progress toward your vision or ideal for your life without first confronting where you currently are. It might be uncomfortable, but the reality is, if you don't acknowledge the gap between where you are and where you want to be, you will never know how to move forward. This is just as true for a person as it is for a society. Whether you're trying to close the gap between American ideals and realities, or your own personal ideals and realities, the first step is acknowledgment.

So, how do we know when we are giving up versus when we are moving on? The distinction between the two lies in one critical question: Is the willingness to grow or improve still there?

If the answer is no—if you find that you or the people involved are no longer willing to grow, change, or evolve—then moving on is not giving up. It's making space for what's next. Whether in a job, a relationship, or a personal pursuit, the moment growth becomes stagnant, and the only thing holding you in place is fear of the unknown, it's time to move on. Growth is the signal that there is still something to be done. When that growth ceases, we must recognize that holding on can prevent us from reaching the next stage of our journey.

Life itself is about growth—we are growing older by the second. By our very nature, mortal death represents the end of physical growth. And just as our physical lives have a natural endpoint, so do other aspects of life. Relationships, careers, and even dreams can reach a point of "death," where their potential for growth is exhausted. In this way, death teaches us more about life than life itself ever can. It reminds us that when growth stops, something must come to an end. But endings, as final as they seem, are not failures. They are transitions. They create space for renewal, for rebirth, for new life to flourish in another form.

In the case of leaving the White House, I could have seen it as giving up on a monumental role. But in reality, staying would have meant holding on to a season that had already served its purpose. Moving on didn't diminish the significance of my contributions—it allowed me to step into the next chapter with faith and purpose. Growth had ceased in that role, and rather than resist the natural end of that chapter, I chose to embrace the promise of what was to come. Just as we must recognize when it's time to move forward in our own lives, the same principle applies to the systems and structures we build. We can't keep clinging to the familiar simply because it's comfortable. True progress— whether personal or societal—requires the courage to release what was in order to step into what could be.

On a broader level, the same principle applies to society. When progress stalls, when growth stops, we must be willing to move on from outdated systems, structures, and at times, even leaders who no longer serve their original purpose. The American ideals of liberty, justice, and equality are timeless, but the way we pursue them must change as society evolves. Clinging to systems that have outlived their usefulness holds us back from the growth we need to close the gap between American ideals and American realities.

On a personal level, the same is true. You can have a dream or an ideal for your life, but if the willingness to grow toward that dream is no longer there, it may be time to reevaluate. Ask yourself: Am I staying in this job, relationship, or mindset because I believe it still has the potential to help me grow, or am I afraid to move on because it's all I know? Growth is the signal that there is still something to be done, but if you've outgrown your current situation, holding on can prevent you from stepping into something greater.

> *Growth is the signal that there is still something to be done.*

Step 1: Acknowledge the Fear

The first step in moving on is to confront the fear of doing so. Fear often masquerades as practicality, convincing us that staying in a familiar place is safer than stepping out into the unknown. But fear is a double-edged sword. It can protect us from harm, yes, but it can also keep us stuck in a place of complacency.

What are you afraid of losing? Is it comfort, routine, or even a sense of identity tied to where you are? Is it a job that defines you, a relationship that feels safe, or a societal norm that no longer serves its original purpose? Acknowledging your fear doesn't mean letting it control you—it means shining a light on the obstacles so that you can move through them.

For our nation, this means confronting the fear of change. What are we, as a society, afraid of losing? Is it the comfort of familiarity, the identity tied to historical norms, or the fear of challenging systems that have been in place for generations? Acknowledging these fears is the first step toward addressing the deep disparities between American ideals and American realities.

On an individual level, what's holding you back from moving forward toward your own personal growth or ideals? Is it the fear of failure, the fear of leaving what's comfortable, or the fear of stepping into an unknown future? The first step in bridging the gap between your personal ideals and realities is to confront the fear that keeps you in place.

Step 2: Reframe Your Perspective

When you're on the verge of giving up, it can feel like you're walking away from everything you've worked for. Moving on isn't walking away from the past—it's making space for the future. This was the revelation Pastor Furtick's sermon brought to me: You might miss today's miracle if you're still holding on to yesterday's blessing.

Are you holding on to something from your past that's preventing you from embracing what's next? A job you've outgrown, a relationship that has run its course, a dream that no longer aligns with who you are today? The price of holding on too tightly is missing out on the new opportunities, experiences, and growth that God has for you in the future. Reframing your perspective helps you see that moving on is not a loss—it's an invitation to step into something greater.

This is also true on a societal level. As a nation, are we holding on to ideals of the past in ways that prevent us from moving forward? The ideals of liberty, justice, and equality are noble, but are we clinging to the outdated methods of pursuing them? To close the gap between American ideals and American realities, we must be willing to let go of approaches that have ceased to produce meaningful growth and embrace new ways of achieving those same ideals.

This is not about giving up on America's foundational principles—it's about making space for a new era of progress. Reframing our perspective as a society allows us to see that true growth and progress are not about abandoning our ideals but about embracing the ways they can evolve to serve all people better. The same applies to personal growth: Moving on from a job, a relationship, or a belief that no longer aligns with your true self doesn't diminish the value of where you've been. It honors your past while making space for the promise of the future.

Step 3: Surround Yourself with Growth

Moving on requires more than just a mental shift, it requires action. One of the most practical ways to ensure you're not giving up but moving on is to surround yourself with people and environments that encourage growth. Growth doesn't happen in isolation. Just like a seed planted in the soil, growth requires nurturing, the right conditions, and an environment that allows it to thrive.

Even though a seed might seem isolated beneath the surface, so much more is happening around it to help it reach its full potential. The soil, the nutrients, the rain, the sunlight, the oxygen—none of these elements work in isolation. The seed depends on its surroundings to flourish. In the same way, we can't grow if we remain in environments that limit us. We need people who pour into us, challenge us, and push us toward growth. Without these external influences, we remain buried, never sprouting into the fullness of what we were created to become.

This same principle applies to societies. If a nation clings to environments, structures, or systems that stifle growth and progress, it will remain stagnant, unable to move forward. Societies must surround themselves with voices, policies, and leaders who foster real growth—who are willing to challenge outdated norms and encourage the kind of progress that closes the gap between ideals and realities.

Personally, surrounding yourself with the right influences is critical to growth. You cannot grow if you are surrounded by people who are comfortable with complacency, or who hold you in a place where growth is no longer possible. If you're not moving forward, ask yourself: Who am I allowing to influence my growth?

As John C. Maxwell teaches in his book *The 15 Invaluable Laws of Growth*, "If you want to grow, you have to be willing to walk away from the things that are no longer helping you reach your full potential." This could be relationships that no longer serve your growth, environments that limit your thinking, or mindsets that keep you stuck. When growth stops, it's a sign that something in your environment must change.

If you find yourself stagnant, take inventory of the people and environments around you. Are they pushing you forward, or are they keeping you stuck? The same is true for societies: Are the systems we've built fostering growth and progress, or are they holding us back from achieving the ideals we espouse?

―――――――

Step 4: Embrace the Process of Moving On

The decision to move on isn't always a single moment—it's a process. It takes time to untangle your identity from the things you're leaving behind. Whether it's a career, a relationship, or even a long-held belief, the process of moving on requires patience, grace, and faith.

Sometimes moving on means trusting that even though you don't see the full picture yet, God has already made a way. The steps you take today, however small they may seem, are leading you toward something greater. Moving on doesn't happen overnight, but each step forward is an act of faith, trusting that what lies ahead is worth the price you're paying by letting go.

On a broader level, societal progress requires embracing the process of moving on from outdated systems and practices. Just as individuals must release what no longer serves them, societies must be willing to confront the structures, policies, and norms that are holding back growth and preventing us from realizing the ideals of liberty, equality, and justice for all.

The key is not to confuse moving on with giving up. Giving up often comes from a place of exhaustion, frustration, or fear, where we throw in the towel because the challenge feels too overwhelming. Moving on, however, comes from a place of growth, wisdom, and discernment—it's the recognition that staying where you are is no longer serving your purpose.

When you're tempted to give up, pause and ask yourself: Am I simply tired, or is this truly no longer where I'm supposed to be? The answer will guide you. If the challenge before you still sparks a desire to grow, then it's worth persevering. But if the only thing keeping you there is fear, then it's time to move on.

The same question applies to our society. Are we holding on to systems and structures because they still serve the purpose of growth, or are we holding on out of fear of change? True progress, both personal and societal, requires knowing when it's time to let go and trust in the process of moving on.

=====

In life, the line between giving up and moving on isn't always clear. It's a space filled with questions, uncertainties, and sometimes, fear.

How do you know if it's time to persevere or if moving forward is the act of faith you need to take? This decision is deeply personal, but it starts with clarity—an honest look at where you are and what's holding you in place.

Tool: Are You Giving Up or Moving On?

The following tool is designed to help you assess whether you are giving up prematurely or if it's time to move on to something new. Are you holding on because there's still growth or because you're afraid to let go? There's no right or wrong answers—only an opportunity to discover what's true for you in this moment and finding courage to act on it.

For each statement, rate yourself on a scale from 1 to 5, where:

1 = Not at all true

3 = Somewhat true

5 = Absolutely true

Statement	Your Rating (1–5)	What This Tells You
I feel **at peace** where I currently am.		A high score means you feel aligned and at ease. A low score suggests internal restlessness or unease.
I am staying because **I believe in this**, not because I fear leaving.		A high score means you are here by choice, not by fear. A low score suggests you may be staying out of obligation or uncertainty.

I sense that **I have outgrown this space**, but I'm hesitant to move forward.		A high score means you feel a shift happening but are unsure how to step into it. A low score suggests you still feel there's growth left in this season.
Moving on **feels more like relief** than regret.		A high score means your spirit feels lighter at the thought of moving on. A low score suggests you may still feel a sense of unfinished work.
Holding on is costing me my peace, joy, or growth.		A high score means staying is draining you. A low score suggests that you still find value and fulfillment in your current space.
TOTAL:		

UNDERSTANDING YOUR RESULTS
Total up your score and compare it to the breakdown below.

20–25 Points: It's Time to Move Forward
You already know that your season here is ending. Holding on any longer may be keeping you from what's next. You've acknowledged that there's little room for growth left in your current situation, and moving forward will open new doors and possibilities. Trust that what you're stepping into will be greater than what you're leaving behind. Fear will try to convince you to stay, but faith is nudging you forward. Listen to that nudge.

13–19 Points: You're in a Season of Discernment
You may still have unfinished work here, or you may be on the edge of something new but not fully ready to step forward. There may

still be lessons to learn, growth to experience, or clarity that needs to come. Take time to pray, seek wise counsel, and pay attention to the signs. The question isn't just whether you're ready to move on—it's whether God is calling you to move now. Trust that when the time is right, the path forward will become unmistakably clear. But first, you have to get still enough and quiet enough to hear.

5–12 Points: Holding On Is the Right Choice—For Now

You're still growing in this space. There is more to be done, more to build, more to refine. Don't rush the process. Sometimes we mistake restlessness for a calling to leave when, in reality, it's an invitation to grow right where we are. Stay engaged, keep learning, and allow yourself to be shaped in this season. When it's truly time to move on, it won't feel like a forced decision—it will feel like a divine release.

UNDERSTANDING THE DIFFERENCE

This tool is meant to guide you toward clarity about your current situation. Whether you're at a crossroads or just contemplating change, understanding the difference between giving up and moving on will help you make a decision rooted in purpose.

Additional Reflection Exercise: Rate Your Readiness to Move On

Now that you've completed the assessment, take a moment to rate your own readiness to move on. For each question, rate yourself from **1 to 5**, where **1** means **"Not Ready"** and **5** means **"Completely Ready."** Afterward, reflect on what your rating tells you about where you stand.

Question	Your Rating (1–5)	What This Tells You
How willing am I to leave my comfort zone?		The more ready you are to move on, the higher your rating should be.
Do I feel excited about new possibilities?		Feeling excitement about change signals readiness to embrace it.
How ready am I to let go of the past?		A high score suggests you're ready to release what was and free yourself for what's next.
Can I envision myself in a new role/space?		A strong sense of vision shows you're prepared to move on.
Am I willing to take a step of faith?		Readiness to act despite fear shows true willingness to embrace new opportunities.
TOTAL:		

INTERPRETING YOUR SCORE

Now that you've rated your readiness, reflect on what your score reveals about where you stand in this season.

20–25 Points: You're Positioned for a New Chapter

Your score reflects a deep internal readiness. The discomfort, restlessness, and **repeated confirmations you've received aren't just passing thoughts—they're signs**. Something greater is calling you forward, and **the only thing left to do is take the step**. The unknown is always intimidating, but trust that what's ahead isn't just different—it's better.

13–19 Points: You're on the Edge of a Decision

You sense that change is coming, but you're still processing the timing. There may be loose ends to tie up, growth to complete, or a final confirmation you're waiting on. If clarity still feels just out of reach, lean into **discernment, patience, and prayer**. The right door will open when you're fully prepared to walk through it.

5–12 Points: Stay Where You Are—For Now

Your season here isn't finished yet. There's still something valuable for you to receive, contribute, or refine. If you're feeling tension, it may not be a sign to leave—it may be an invitation to **lean in**. Growth isn't always comfortable, but it's necessary. Instead of looking ahead, focus on deepening your roots where you are. When the time to move comes, you'll know.

Your score isn't about telling you what to do—it's about helping you recognize what you already know deep down. Whether your next step is staying, discerning, or stepping forward, trust that **clarity comes when we quiet the noise, lean into truth, and listen** to what faith has been whispering all along.

―――――

Faith in the Unknown

What's keeping you from moving on? Is it fear, comfort, or a desire to hold on to what was? I want to encourage you: Don't let the fear of the unknown keep you from stepping into what's next. Moving on is not the same as giving up—it's an act of faith, an acknowledgment that your journey isn't finished. It's a step toward growth, toward the future, and toward the fulfillment of your purpose.

The same principle applies to closing the gap between societal ideals and realities. Moving on from systems that no longer serve their purpose isn't about abandoning the ideals that shaped us—it's about embracing the opportunity to live up to them more fully. It's about stepping forward in faith, believing that progress is possible, and trusting that growth will come as we evolve and adapt.

When I was appointed as the first-ever Chief Diversity and Inclusion Officer at the White House, it was a pioneering moment—not just for me but for the institution itself. It was a role that had never existed before, a position that God had created for me to step into. While that chapter has now closed, it was a powerful reminder of this truth: When you make room for God, God will create rooms for you. Sometimes those rooms require us to move on from what's familiar, to step out of what's comfortable, and to trust that God is preparing something even greater ahead.

The price of giving up is the weight of regret—the what-ifs that haunt us when we know we've stopped short of our potential. But the promise of moving on is the freedom to embrace new possibilities, new miracles that God has waiting for us. Just like Pastor Furtick said, holding on to yesterday's blessings can prevent you from receiving today's miracles.

Remember: Moving on doesn't erase the value of where you've been. It honors it by recognizing that your story is still being written, and the best is yet to come. Let go of the fear, the comfort, the past, and step forward into the promise that lies ahead—for yourself, for your community, and for a society that is ready to move closer to the ideals we all hold dear.

As you prepare to take the next step, consider this: Fear will always be present at moments of decision. It is a constant companion on the path to purpose. But faith, when truly embraced, doesn't just carry you beyond fear. It silences it because faith reminds you of this truth: What is ahead is greater than what you are leaving behind. The only question is, will you trust the promise more than the price? It is there, in the space between fear and faith, that your next chapter isn't just waiting. It's calling.

CHAPTER 14

The Choice That Changes Everything

WHICH IS MORE IMPORTANT: WHERE YOU WERE WHEN YOU took your first breath or where you will be when you take your last? The answer lies somewhere in between those two sacred moments—everything that happens between your first breath and your last. Every choice, every step forward or backward, is the measure of your life. In those moments, fear and faith wrestle for dominance, shaping the path you choose to take.

Fear is a master of disguise. It doesn't always announce itself loudly; it whispers in the quietest corners of our minds. It shows up as hesitation when we're about to take a risk, as doubt when we're close to success, and as excuses when we're faced with hard truths. Fear is clever—it convinces us that holding back is safer, that playing small is wise. Its cost is immeasurable, robbing us not just of opportunities but of the fullness of who we're meant to become. But faith—the conviction to move even when you cannot see the next step—carries the promise of transformation.

Every story I've shared with you throughout this book has been a testimony to the ongoing battle between faith and fear. Fear crept into my heart at every major crossroads in the process of writing this very book. I feared writing the wrong thing. I feared sharing too much or too little. I feared what others might think. But time and again, God reminded me: This journey is an act of faith. The same is true in life—fear always appears when we are closest to stepping fully into what we are called to do. What if faith spoke louder?

Fear is often the hidden force behind division, missed potential, the reluctance to follow your purpose, and the unwillingness to move on. It sneaks in and shapes our lives in ways we don't even realize until it's too late. It makes us question our worth, second-guess our talents, and ultimately, hold back from taking the necessary steps forward. Faith—the belief in something greater, the willingness to leap even when you cannot see the ground beneath you—demands the opposite. Faith invites us to stretch beyond our comfort zones, to face the unknown head-on, trusting that the steps we take will lead us to where we need to go.

Many of us are paralyzed by fear, taking steps we aren't graced for, pushing forward on paths not meant for us. Yet when we are closest to fulfilling our purpose—when we are on the cusp of becoming who we are meant to be—that's when fear strikes hardest. It tries to convince us that we are not enough, that the price of moving forward is too high. But what we must realize is that *fear is always costly*. Fear is what keeps us stuck, prevents growth, and stunts progress in ways we may not even be aware of until years down the line.

The price of fear can be subtle, like the missed opportunity to speak up in a meeting, or profound, like the decision to stay in a job, a relationship, or a situation that no longer serves us. But the price of fear is not just what we miss—it's the parts of ourselves we suppress, the pieces of our potential that remain unexpressed. Fear's cost isn't just external; it's deeply internal, often robbing us of our peace, our joy, and our sense of purpose.

Think about the moments when fear has dictated your choices. What did it cost you? How many times did it make you doubt your worth or silence your voice? Fear doesn't just take opportunities—it takes pieces of your confidence, leaving your potential unexplored and your spirit diminished.

When we let fear drive our lives, we play small. We tell ourselves that we're being "practical" or "realistic," but really, we're just afraid. Afraid of failure, afraid of rejection, afraid of what others might think. Here's the thing: Fear never stays contained. It spreads. It seeps into every corner of our lives, affecting not just the big decisions, but the small ones, too. The longer we let fear control us, the more it costs us.

Nevertheless, faith offers a different kind of promise. It invites us to step into the unknown, not with the guarantee of success, but with the promise of growth. Faith doesn't erase fear; it helps us to move forward despite it. It says, "Yes, this is scary. Yes, you might fail. But take the step anyway."

Faith requires trust. Trust that even though the path is unclear, the journey itself will bring clarity. It's about believing that every step forward, no matter how uncertain, is a step closer to your purpose. Faith is not about avoiding fear—it's about confronting it and choosing to move forward anyway.

Faith is the key to unlocking your fullest potential. It is the force that allows you to see past your current circumstances and into the future that awaits you. Faith is what enables you to take risks, to try new things, to push beyond your comfort zone. It's what makes transformation possible. And while fear keeps us tethered to what we know, faith propels us into the unknown, where growth and possibility reside.

Faith asks for something simple, yet profound: trust. It requires you to trust that even though you can't predict the outcome, even though the road ahead might be unclear, the journey itself will bring clarity. The promise of faith is not the absence of challenges, but the presence of growth through those challenges.

> *Faith asks for something simple, yet profound: trust.*

Faith is a choice you must make again and again, in the small moments and the big ones. It's not a one-time decision. It's an ongoing commitment to step forward, even when the path ahead seems uncertain. Just as fear and faith shape our individual lives, they also define the trajectory of our communities and nations. What we choose in our personal moments of decision ripples outward, influencing the world around us. Faith is what carries us beyond the limitations we've placed on ourselves, aligning us with our true purpose. The same battle plays out on a much larger scale. Just as fear can keep us small as individuals, it can also keep entire societies from evolving.

It is imperative to remember that faith is not just about the individual—it's about something greater. It's a collective call, a shared belief in the power of what we can accomplish together. Faith holds the potential to transform not only our personal lives but also the societies in which we live. It has the power to shift nations, to close the gap between ideals and realities. What if we made the courageous choice, today, to replace fear with faith— not as an abstract ideal, but as a deliberate and transformative act? Our world depends on it. Imagine what could be accomplished if we stepped forward together, united in our belief that something greater is possible.

Think about the state of our world. Division persists. Inequity remains entrenched. Societies wrestle with challenges that feel insurmountable—systemic injustices, economic disparities, climate crises. The enormity of these issues tempts us to retreat, to surrender to fear, to believe the lie that change is beyond our reach.

But what if, instead, we leaned into the collective power of faith? Faith in progress. Faith in justice. Faith in our ability to rise above the obstacles and rewrite what feels unchangeable.

America, like much of the world, has always wrestled with the gap between its founding ideals and the lived realities of its people. Liberty. Equality. Justice. These words are often spoken, but the work of aligning them with reality demands more than rhetoric—it demands courage, action, and faith. Here's the truth: Closing this gap doesn't rest solely on the shoulders of a few leaders or institutions. It requires all of us—not some of us—to take part.

The path to meaningful change doesn't begin on a grand stage or in the halls of power—it begins in the quiet, ordinary moments of our daily lives. If we want to see change on a national level, it starts at the local level. The decisions we make in our homes, our schools, our workplaces, and our communities ripple outward in ways we cannot always see. Faith has the power to spark those ripples and, in time, create waves of change. The courage to choose faith, to believe in the possibility of progress, is what turns those ripples into a tide that reshapes the future.

This isn't just about America. This truth applies to every nation, every community, every corner of the world. Progress is not permanent, and neither is the time we are given to create it. The window to act is fleeting, but the legacy we leave behind can endure. What will that legacy be? Will we cling to fear, allowing it to keep us tethered to outdated systems, or will we step forward in faith, daring to believe in a future that reflects the best of who we are?

The choice is ours. The power to close the gap lies not in distant, abstract forces, but in our collective hands. Every conversation, vote, and act of kindness becomes part of the ripple effect that reshapes the future. Every act of faith—every decision to love instead of hate, to build instead of destroy, to lift others up instead of leaving them behind—moves us closer to the world we dream of. This is the promise of faith: the power to create a future where ideals are not just spoken, but lived.

The Moment of Choice

Here's the ultimate truth: Fear and faith both require something of you. They both ask you to believe in something that hasn't happened yet. But only one leads to fulfillment. Only one path brings you closer to who you are meant to be. The other keeps you bound to what could have been. You've already seen this play out in your life. The decisions you didn't make. The words you didn't say. The opportunities that passed you by because fear whispered louder than faith. But what if you decided, right now, that fear would no longer dictate your story?

What if you chose faith?—not as a fleeting feeling but as a guiding force? Faith that the step you're afraid to take holds the key to a future beyond your imagination. The unknown is not a void to fear but a doorway to discovery.

Faith is the connection between your aspirations and your actions, the force that transforms unseen possibilities into lived realities. It gives you the courage to leave behind what no longer serves you and step boldly into the life that's waiting for you.

The choice is yours. Faith and fear both live in the realm of the unseen, but only faith will carry you toward the life you were meant to live. And every time you choose faith, you become the author of your own story, rewriting the pages that fear once held captive.

I hope you reflect on the story you've been writing with your life. Every step you take in faith is a step toward the life you were always meant to live. Don't let fear be the author of your future. Embrace the unknown, trust the journey, and believe that the best is not just ahead—it's within your reach, waiting for you to claim it.

Remember this: Whatever you are not changing, you are choosing. Faith and fear both ask you to believe in the unseen, but only faith offers you the promise of transformation. Faith is what gives you the power to rewrite your story, to turn the page, and to continue writing the masterpiece of your life.

So, as you stand at the crossroads of faith and fear, the question isn't merely, "What will happen if I take the leap?" It's something far deeper: "What will I lose if I don't?" What chapter in your life is fear keeping you from writing? What potential remains unrealized because you're afraid to pick up the pen? What dreams will fade into regret, what relationships will remain only possibilities, and what opportunities will never see the light of day because fear whispered louder than faith?

The choice before you isn't just about stepping forward—it's about reclaiming your agency. Will you let fear dictate the chapters yet to be written, or will you rise above, embracing the courage to create a story that only you can tell? This is your moment to decide—not just who you are, but who you are becoming.

Time will tell the story of your life. The decisions you make today will ripple into tomorrow, shaping the days, months, and years ahead. Here's what I believe with all my heart: Time will tell a beautiful story—a story of courage, resilience, and the quiet strength it took to rise above fear and walk in faith. Your story will be a testament to the beauty of choosing growth, even when it felt uncertain.

I hope to meet you somewhere along this journey. One day, perhaps our paths will cross, and we'll look back on this moment—this sacred pause between what was and what could be—and celebrate the steps you took. The steps

Time will tell the story of your life.

that moved you closer to your purpose, closer to becoming the person you've always been destined to be. But until that day comes, live boldly, love deeply, and walk forward in faith. Every decision, every step, no matter how small, is a line written in the extraordinary story of your life. And here's the truth: You hold the pen.

The world is waiting—not for perfection, but for the light that only you carry. Step forward, not in fear but in faith. Trust that each step you take, no matter how uncertain, is part of a plan greater than you can imagine. Know this: The best isn't just ahead—it's already within you. All this time, while you've been waiting for your moment, your moment has been waiting for you.

Acknowledgments

First and foremost, I give thanks to God the Father, Jesus Christ the Son, and the Holy Spirit for being my source of faith, hope, and love. Without Your presence, none of this would have been possible.

To my wife, Brittany—your love, wisdom, and unwavering support have been my anchor. Thank you for your patience, sacrifice, and belief in me, even on the most challenging days. Your strength, grace, and faith inspire me daily, and I am beyond grateful to walk this journey of life with you. You are my greatest blessing.

To my twin daughters, Lela and Nia, my prayer is that this book will one day serve as a reminder that faith is greater than fear and that you are capable of anything with God's guidance. Always know that I love you, I am proud of you, and I will always be with you. And for whenever you have future moments of doubt, always remember who you are and whose you are. Know that comparison is the death of joy—the only person you need to be better than is the one you were yesterday. Keep your faith strong, your hearts open, and your purpose clear, knowing that you were created for something greater than you can even imagine.

To my parents, Mitchell and Maria Leach, thank you for the foundation of faith you laid for me to walk on and for teaching me the value of perseverance, love, and humility. To my brothers,

Mitchell Leach II and Martell Leach, your unwavering support, encouragement, and love have been a constant source of strength. To my extended Leach family and Jones family—thank you for your steadfast love, support, and understanding throughout this journey. To the Wharton family—Brittany's family—thank you for your unyielding love and support throughout this journey. Your support has meant more than words can express.

To my agent, Scott Kaufman, who believed in this vision and guided me through every step of this process, I am forever grateful. To the entire Buchwald team, your belief in me has been invaluable.

To Angela Guzman of HarperOne—your diligence, creativity, and thoughtful feedback have shaped this story into something I am truly proud of. I could not have asked for a better partner for telling this story. To the entire HarperCollins Publishers team— thank you for your commitment and care in bringing this book to life.

To every pastor and faith leader who has built my faith and prayed for me along the way, your influence has been immeasurable. To the church communities I've been blessed to be part of throughout the years, thank you for your fellowship, encouragement, and the shared faith that has continually strengthened me and made me better.

To my friends, who are like family, thank you for walking with me through every season and for your honest feedback on the early drafts of this book. A special thank you to Lester McCarroll III— your steadfast friendship and support throughout this journey have made a difference.

To the 2020 presidential campaign team I was fortunate to be a part of and the forty-sixth presidential administration staff I served alongside—thank you for inspiring me with your commitment to service and for the lessons I learned in those historic spaces. To the

Miami Dolphins, Chicago Bears, the NFL, and my alma maters, the University of Illinois at Urbana-Champaign and St. Thomas University (Miami, Florida), thank you for shaping the person I've become.

And to you, the reader—whether this book is in your hands for the first time or the fifth—I thank you for your curiosity and your trust. I didn't know who would open this book or when, but I knew God did. Thank you for your interest and for the contribution you'll make to the world after reading these pages. I trust this book will add value to your life, just as it has to mine in writing it.

Finally, to everyone who believed in this vision and made it a reality, know that this is as much your story as it is mine—thank you. Your belief has helped carry this story forward, and I hope it inspires others for years to come.

Notes

Chapter 2: From Passed Over to Passover

41 *three key seasons on God's calendar:* Steve Munsey, *Seven Blessings of the Atonement* (Refuge Productions, 2008).

41 *He taught that these three feast seasons:* Munsey, *Seven Blessings.*

Chapter 3: Taking a Stand: The Kaepernick Effect

68 *Speaking at a news conference:* "Press Conference by President Obama after G20 Summit," the White House, September 5, 2016, https://obamawhitehouse .archives.gov/the-press-office/2016/09/05/press-conference-president-obama -after-g20-summit.

70 *Trump declared:* "President Trump Remarks at Senator Strange Campaign Rally," C-SPAN, September 22, 2017, https://www.c-span.org/video /?434480-1/president-trump-remarks-senator-strange-campaign-rally.

Chapter 7: The Wake-Up Call

126 *Prolapsed umbilical cords:* "Prolapsed Umbilical Cord: Obstetric Emergency," *American Journal of Obstetrics and Gynecology*, 105, no. 4 (1969): 409–17.

126 *Black maternal health disparities:* Centers for Disease Control and Prevention, "Racial and Ethnic Disparities Continue in Pregnancy-Related Deaths," September 5, 2019, https://archive.cdc.gov/www_cdc_gov/media /releases/2019/p0905-racial-ethnic-disparities-pregnancy-deaths.html.

134 *As the nation grows more diverse:* "Demographic Turning Points for the United States: Population Projections for 2020 to 2060," United States Census Bureau, February 2020, https://www.census.gov/library/publications /2020/demo/p25-1144.html.

Chapter 10: From Division to Unity

171 *Studies have shown:* Julianne Holt-Lunstad, Timothy B. Smith, and J. Bradley Layton, "Social Relationships and Mortality Risk: A Meta-analytic Review," *PLoS Medicine* 7, no. 7 (2010): e1000316, https://doi.org/10.1371/journal.pmed.1000316.

171 *Research conducted by Harvard's:* Giulia Cambieri, "The Importance of Connections: Ways to Live a Longer, Healthier Life," Harvard T. H. Chan School of Public Health, December 8, 2024, https://hsph.harvard.edu/news/the-importance-of-connections-ways-to-live-a-longer-healthier-life/.

About the Author

Michael Leach is a distinguished leader whose career spans the NFL, national politics, and the White House. He began his professional journey in the National Football League, serving as Assistant to the Head Coach for the Chicago Bears before later managing labor relations at NFL headquarters. In 2020, he served as Chief People Officer and Head of Diversity and Inclusion for the Biden-Harris presidential campaign, helping lead and build the most diverse general election campaign staff in US history—before ultimately making history in 2021 as the first-ever Chief Diversity and Inclusion Officer and as Special Assistant to the President. Today, Michael is the founder and CEO of BridgeTrust Partners, a consulting firm specializing in tailored advisory services, partnership cultivation, leadership development, public speaking, event hosting, and grant management services. His team is dedicated to fostering powerful collaborations that drive innovation, elevate purpose, and spark cultural transformation across industries. Now, entering the literary and entertainment worlds, Michael is committed to inspiring, equipping, and empowering people through story-rich content, live experiences, and transformational conversations that meet the moment—and move the masses.

Next Steps and Resources

Keep Building Beyond the Book

JOIN THE *FAITH OVER FEAR* COMMUNITY

Scan the code or visit MyFaithOverFear.com to dive deeper into *Faith Over Fear*. Access behind-the-scenes insights, exclusive interviews, curated articles, and tools to accelerate your growth. Connect with a community—online and in person—built around resilience, purpose, and shared faith, and be the first to know about events and new content that empower you to choose faith over fear.

DISCOVER BRIDGETRUST PARTNERS

Scan the code or visit BridgeTrustPartners.com to learn how BridgeTrust Partners—a strategic consulting and storytelling firm at the intersection of business, culture, and social change—can partner with YOU. Through leadership advising, partnership cultivation, stakeholder-engagement strategy, executive search (for organizations filling mission-critical roles or talent seeking life-changing opportunities), and public speaking, we equip teams to transform culture and drive lasting impact.